PHYTOCHEMICALS AND BIOACTIVITY

A SIMPLE GUIDE TO RESEARCHERS WHO INTERESTED IN PHYTOCHEMICALS

DR. A. CHARLES | DR. C. GOPI | DR. P. ADWIN JOSE

Made with ♥ on the Notion Press Platform
www.notionpress.com

"I'd like to dedicate my work to my Parents"

Dedicate To My Parents

Contents

Foreword

Welcome to the book of Phytochemicals and Bio-Activity. This textbook has been created with several goals in mind: accessibility, customization and engagement of young researcher, master degree students etc., This Book explains and focused the Phenomenal growth of modern chemical and biological science has created new awareness in the unlimited potential of the natural products from plants. Today, the natural products derived from plants are being tested for the new modes of pharmacological actions such as to be the new drugs. A special characteristic of some of the higher plants is their capacity to produce a large number of metabolites especially the secondary metabolites.

Recent studies are focused on the isolation and identification of new therapeutic compounds from higher plants for their medicinal properties of healing certain diseases. In India, a large number of plant species had been screened for their pharmacological properties. But, an appreciable number of endangered species had to be explored, yet. Medicinal plants are of great interest to the field of biotechnology, as most of the drug industries depend on these plant-metabolites for the production of a number of pharmaceutical compounds.

Many drugs commonly used today are of herbal origin because of their safety, quality and efficacy. Herbal drugs, nutraceuticals, food supplements, folk medicines, pharmaceutical intermediates and new chemical entities. Sweeteners, flavor, fragrances, pigments and a number of health care related products from plant origin

Preface

The subject of Phytochemistry, or plant chemistry, has developed in recent years as a distinct discipline. It is somewhere in between material product organic chemistry and plant biochemistry. It is closely related to natural products. It deals with the enormous variety of organic substances that are elaborated and accumulated by plants. Also, it deals with the chemical structures of their substances, stereochemistry, dynamic aspects (reaction) their biosynthesis, turnover and metabolism, their natural distribution and their biological function.

'Natural products' in the broadest sense cannot be all the chemical compounds which occur in nature. However, by convention and practice, the term is now used to refer only to the organic compounds occurring in nature. The boundaries are further defined by restricting the term to the primary and secondary metabolites. It focuses on the chemistry of these compounds, and thus keep the subject under the umbrella of organic chemistry.

Medicinal and aromatic plants which act as a well spring of traditional systems of medicine. A medicinal plant was used in India for centuries as an important therapeutic source for treating wide variety of ailments and has been found to be of immense global importance. Many familiar medications of the twenty century were developed from ancient healing traditions that treated health problems with specific plants. Folk medicines are significant source of Ayurvedic, Unani, Traditional Chinese Medicine and Medical herbalism. It incorporates crude medicinal herbs, decoctions and infusions and syrups. Folk medicines are still practiced by some vendors, hakims and vaids in remote areas and some folk preparations are of surprising high curative value.

Plants have almost limitless ability to synthesize aromatic substances mainly secondary metabolites, of which at least 12,000 have been isolated, a number estimated to be less than 10% of the total. Natural products which are produced by plants, have been isolated as biologically active pharmacophores. Approximately one third of the top-selling drugs in the world are natural products or their derivatives often with ethno pharmacological background. The advantage of natural products for random screening is the structural diversity provided by natural products, which is greater than provided by most available combinatorial approaches based on heterocyclic compounds. It is suggested that the ethno-directed sampling which is most likely to succeed in identifying drugs used in the treatment of various illness.

Natural products and their derivatives re including antibiotics represent more than 50% of all drugs in clinical use in the world. Higher plants contribute about 25% of the total. Hence, medicinal plants are believed to be an important source of new chemical substances with potential therapeutic effects.

Phenomenal growth of modern chemical and biological science has created new awareness in the unlimited potential of the natural products from plants. Today, the natural products derived from plants are being tested for the new modes of pharmacological actions such as to be the new drugs. A special characteristic of some of the higher plants is their capacity to produce a large number of metabolites especially the secondary metabolites. Recent studies are focused on the isolation and identification of new therapeutic compounds from higher plants for their medicinal properties of healing certain diseases. In India, a large number of plant species had been screened for their pharmacological properties. But, an appreciable number of endangered species had to be explored, yet. Medicinal plants are of great interest to the field of biotechnology, as most of the drug industries depend on these plant-metabolites for the production of a number of pharmaceutical compounds.

Many drugs commonly used today are of herbal origin because of their safety, quality and efficacy. Herbal drugs, nutraceuticals, food supplements, folk medicines, pharmaceutical intermediates and new chemical entities. Sweeteners, flavor, fragrances, pigments and a number of health care related products from plant origin.

The qualitative and quantitative estimation of the phytochemical constituents of a medicinal plant is considered to be an important step in medicinal plant research. Phytochemical progress has been aided enormously by the development of rapid and accurate methods of screening plants for particular chemicals8. The most important bioactive constituents of the plants come under the class of compounds like alkaloids, terpenoids, phenolic, flavonoids, tannins, quinones, phytosterols, lignans, saponins etc.

Acknowledgements

First I would like to thank our Management of E.G.S. Pillay Engineering College, Nagapattinam, to provide opportunities to complete this research book.

I would like to thank our Principal, E.G.S. Pillay Engineering College, Nagapattinam, for guidance and advice that carried me through all the stages of writing this research book.

I would like to express my sincere thanks to our Academic director for providing encouragement and constant support to me in all stages of writing this research book.

I would like to convey my sincere and deep gratitude to our research Director, for giving me the occasion to give motivation, write this research book, and provide precious guidance up to the completion.

And also I express my special thanks to the Head of the Department, Science and Humanities, E.G.S. Pillay Engineering College, Nagapattinam, for her authentic support throughout this book writing.

I am extending my thanks to all Department Staff members, Science and Humanities, E.G.S. Pillay Engineering College for their valuable help and suggestions throughout the studies.

Finally I would like to give special thanks to my family members as a whole for their continuous support and understanding when undertaking my research and writing this book. Your prayer for me was what sustained me this far.

Prologue

In food science the term ‘phytochemicals’ includes a variety of plant ingredients with different structures that are capable of health-promoting effects. Phytonutrients are natural substances but are not called nutrients in the traditional sense, since they are synthesized by plants neither in energy metabolism nor in anabolic or catabolic metabolism, but only in specific cell types. They differ from primary plant compounds in that they are not essential to the plant. Phytonutrients perform important tasks in the secondary metabolism of plants as repellents to pests and sunlight as well as growth regulators. They occur only in low concentrations and usually have a pharmacological effect. Since antiquity, these effects have been used in naturopathy in the form of medicinal herbs, spices, teas, and foods. With the development of highly sensitive analytical methods, a variety of these substances could be identified. These phytochemicals may have health benefits or adverse health effects, depending on the dosage. In the past, these effects were studied in cell and tissue cultures as well as in animal models. Meanwhile there are numerous epidemiological data that point to the extensive health potential of phytochemicals in humans. A high dietary intake of phytochemicals with vegetables, fruits, nuts, legumes, and whole grain is associated with a reduced risk for cardiovascular and other diseases.

CHAPTER ONE

INTRODUCTION TO PHYTOCHEMICALS AND THEIR BIO ACTIVITY

The subject of Phytochemistry, or plant chemistry, has developed in recent years as a distinct discipline. It is somewhere in between material product organic chemistry and plant biochemistry. It is closely related to natural products. It deals with the enormous variety of organic substances that are elaborated and accumulated by plants. Also, it deals with the chemical structures of their substances, stereochemistry, dynamic aspects (reaction) their biosynthesis, turnover and metabolism, their natural distribution and their biological function [1].

'Natural products' in the broadest sense cannot be all the chemical compounds which occur in nature. However, by convention and practice, the term is now used to refer only to the organic compounds occurring in nature. The boundaries are further defined by restricting the term to the primary and secondary metabolites. It focuses on the chemistry of these compounds, and thus keep the subject under the umbrella of organic chemistry[2].

Medicinal and aromatic plants which act as a well spring of traditional systems of medicine. A medicinal plant was used in India for centuries as an important therapeutic source for treating wide variety of ailments and has been found to be of immense global importance. Many familiar medications of the twenty century were developed from ancient healing traditions that treated health problems with specific plants. Folk medicines are significant source of Ayurvedic, Unani, Traditional Chinese Medicine and Medical herbalism. It incorporates crude medicinal herbs, decoctions and infusions and syrups. Folk medicines are still practiced by some vendors, hakims and vaids in remote areas and some folk preparations are of surprising high curative value3.

Plants have almost limitless ability to synthesize aromatic substances mainly secondary metabolites, of which at least 12,000 have been isolated, a number estimated to be less than 10% of the total. Natural products which are produced by plants, have been isolated as biologically active pharmacophores. Approximately one third of the top-selling drugs in the world are natural products or their derivatives often with ethno pharmacological background. The advantage of natural products for random screening is the structural diversity provided by natural products, which is greater than provided by most available combinatorial approaches based on heterocyclic compounds. It is suggested that the ethno-directed sampling which is most likely to succeed in identifying drugs used in the treatment of various illness. Natural products and their derivatives are including antibiotics represent more than 50% of all drugs in clinical use in the world. Higher plants contribute about 25% of the total. Hence, medicinal plants are believed to be an important source of new chemical substances with potential therapeutic effects [3,4].

Phenomenal growth of modern chemical and biological science has created new awareness in the unlimited potential of the natural products from plants. Today, the natural products derived from plants are being tested for the new modes of pharmacological actions such as to be the new drugs. A special characteristic of some of the higher plants is their capacity to produce a large number of metabolites especially secondary metabolites. Recent studies are focused on the isolation and identification of new therapeutic compounds from higher plants for their medicinal properties of healing certain diseases. In India, a large number of plant species had been screened for their pharmacological properties. But, an appreciable number of endangered species had to be explored, yet. Medicinal plants are of great interest to the field of biotechnology, as most of the drug industries depend on these plant-metabolites for the production of a number of pharmaceutical compounds[5,6].

Many drugs commonly used today are of herbal origin because of their safety, quality and efficacy. Herbal drugs, nutraceuticals, food supplements, folk medicines, pharmaceutical intermediates and new chemical entities. Sweeteners, flavor, fragrances, pigments and a number of health care related products from plant origin[7].

The qualitative and quantitative estimation of the phytochemical constituents of a medicinal plant is considered to be an important step in medicinal plant research. Phytochemical progress has been aided enormously by the development of rapid and accurate methods of screening plants for particular chemicals8. The most important bioactive constituents of the plants come under the class of compounds like alkaloids, terpenoids, phenolic, flavonoids, tannins, quinones, phytosterols, lignans, saponins etc. These natural products are obtained from plant sources by systematic extraction and isolation. They were characterized by general protocol followed by phytochemists to know the active functionality. The whole methodologies given schematically in **Figure 1.1.**

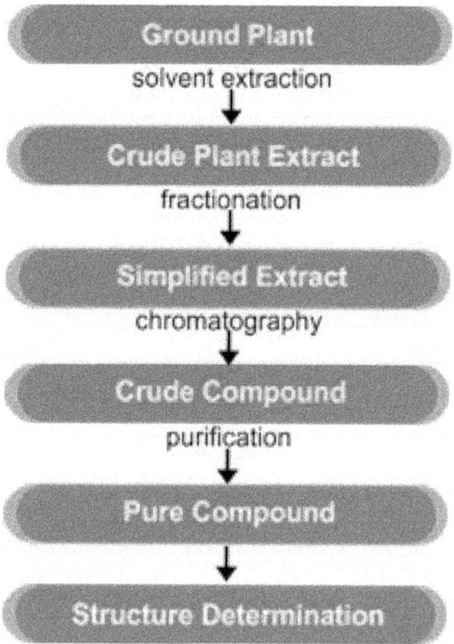

Fig 1.1. General scheme of phytochemical processes followed by Chemist.

The Early method of isolation involved by selective crystallization of the most dominant component in the mixture. Liquid natural products are distilled by super critical fluid extraction. Natural organic acids are isolated by aqueous basic extraction and natural organic bases (alkaloids) are isolated by aqueous acidic extraction. Modern chromatographic methods have been developed greatly to isolate and purify a large number of different compounds in very small quantities like Column, GC, TLC, HPLC, Paper, electrophoresis, ion exchange etc.

To determine the functional groups of isolated compounds by IR and Raman spectroscopy. C-13, DEPT, HMBC NMR spectroscopy are useful to determine the carbon skeleton and the location of the functional groups. Isolated pure compounds are degraded into smaller fragments (A-B-C → A + B + C) in order to determine the molecular mass. Elemental analysis by XRF, colorimetric, flame photometer and AAS. Reactivity of secondary metabolites (leading to new reactions).After deriving the structure of the compound from above mentioned analytical technique, it has been subjected to identify the type of stereo isomers. (Stereochemistry of optically pure compound). Synthesis of the smaller fragments (A, B, C), the entire molecule (A-B-C) and classification of the compound into a biogenetic family. Biosynthetic pathways of primary metabolites leading to secondary metabolites in plants given schematically in **Figure 1.2.**

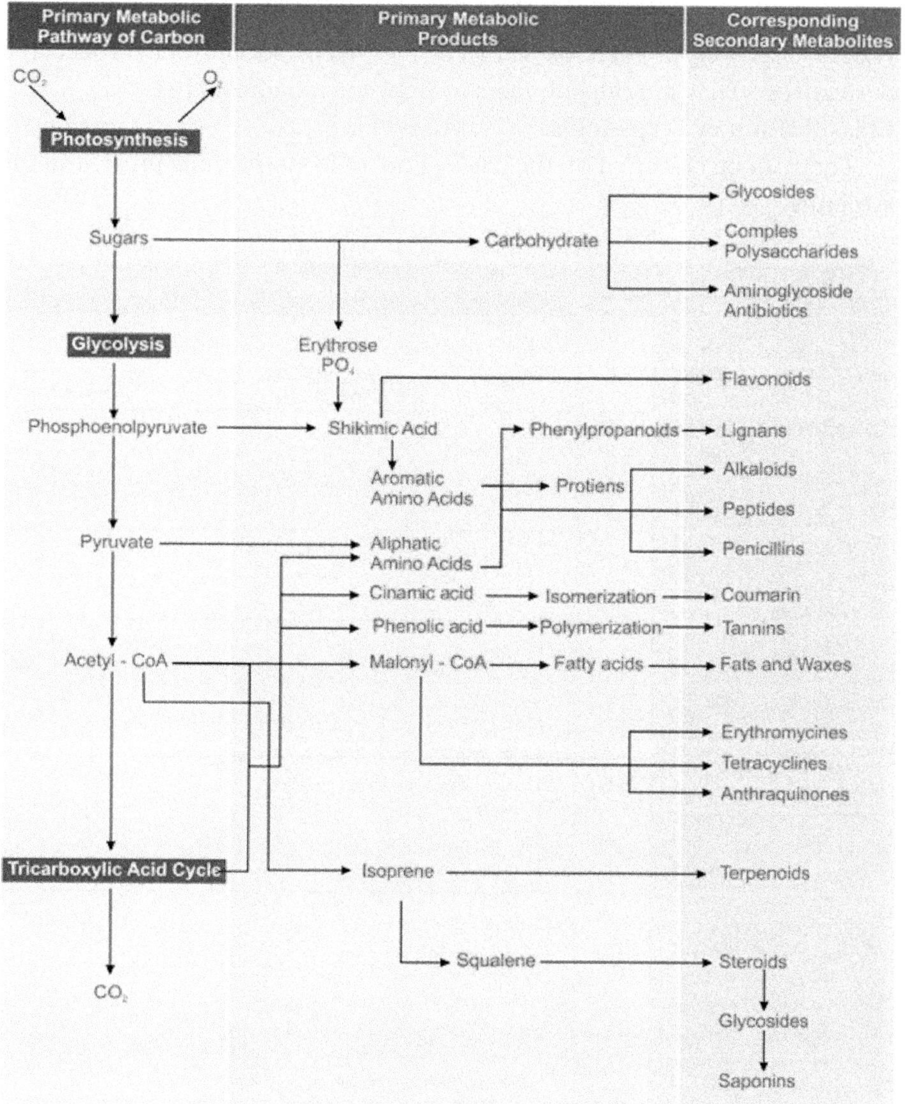

Fig 1.2. Biosynthetic pathways leading to secondary metabolites in plants

Chemistry of Terpenoids.

Terpenoids are volatile substances which give plants and flowers their fragrance. They occur widely in the leaves and fruits of higher plants such as camphor, conifers, citrus and eucalyptus. By the modern definition: "Terpenoids are the hydrocarbons of plant origin of the general formula $(C_5H_8)_n$ as well as their oxygenated, hydrogenated and dehydrogenated derivatives ".They are the polymers of isoprene monomers [8].

Classification of Terpenoids:

They can be classified on the basis of no. of isoprene units present in the structure.

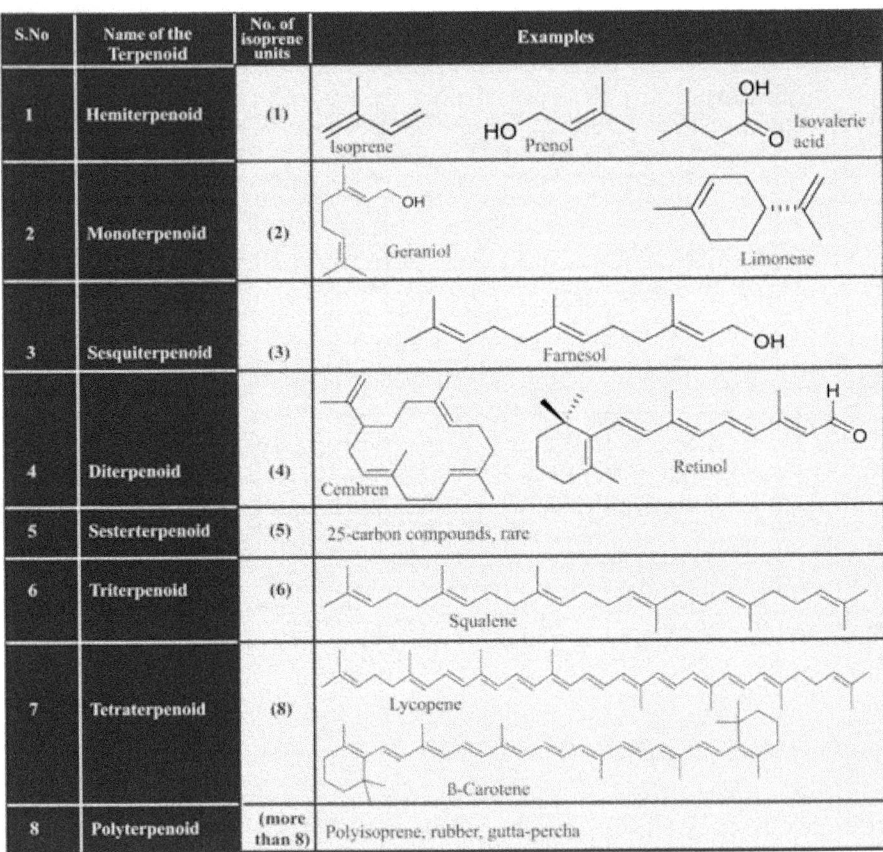

S.No	Name of the Terpenoid	No. of isoprene units	Examples
1	Hemiterpenoid	(1)	Isoprene, Prenol, Isovaleric acid
2	Monoterpenoid	(2)	Geraniol, Limonene
3	Sesquiterpenoid	(3)	Farnesol
4	Diterpenoid	(4)	Cembren, Retinol
5	Sesterterpenoid	(5)	25-carbon compounds, rare
6	Triterpenoid	(6)	Squalene
7	Tetraterpenoid	(8)	Lycopene, B-Carotene
8	Polyterpenoid	(more than 8)	Polyisoprene, rubber, gutta-percha

Table 1. Classification of Terpenoids.

Biogenesis of Terpenoids:

The biosynthesis of terpenoids can be divided into three definite steps is given illustratively in **Figure 3.**

1. The formation of an isopentane unit from acetate.

2. The condensation of this unit to form acyclic terpenoids.
3. The conversion of acyclic terpenoids into cyclic terpenoids and the introduction of functional groups.

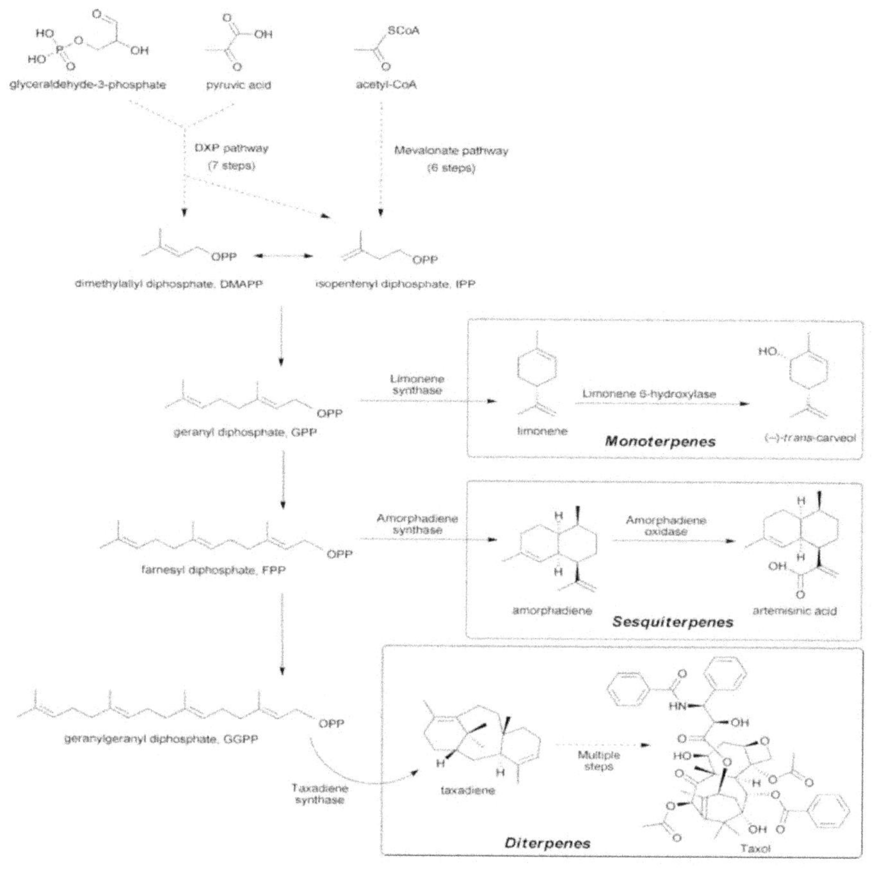

Fig: 3. Biogenesis of Terpenoids

Terpenoids have been attractive constituents and extensive biological investigations have been carried out within the group and some of these studies have revealed that a broad spectrum of pharmacological and physiological properties, some of which have led to a number of terpenoids gaining medicinal application. Few of the simpler naturally-occurring terpenoids are in clinical use today, for their research no so much, perhaps for their commercial or therapeutic importance some of the important bioactive terpenoids compound isolated from plant origin and their molecular structures given below **Table 2.**

S.No.	Name of the terpenoids (types)	Molecular structures	Plant origin/Family	bio-activity
1.	Andrographolide (diterpenoid)	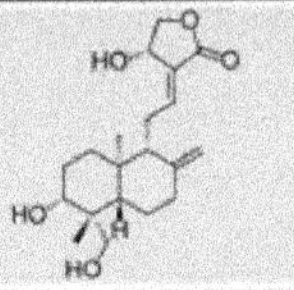	Andrographis paniculata / Acanthaceae	Immunomodulation and stroke.
2.	Camphor (mono terpenoid)	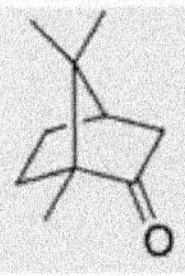	Cinnamomum camphora / Lauraceae	Anesthetic and antimicrobial
3.	Ginkgolides (diterpenoids)	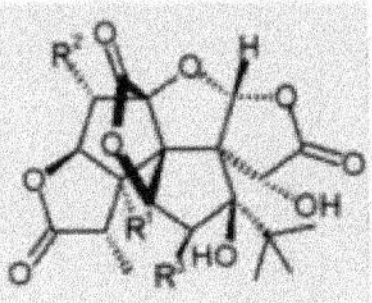	Ginkgo biloba / Ginkgoaceae	Neuroprotective
4.	Zerumbone (sesquiterpene)	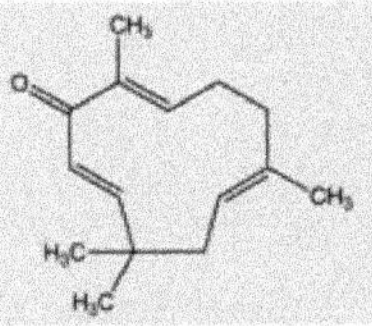	Zingeber amaricans / Zingeberaceae	Anti - microbial /cytotoxic
5.	Quassin (triterpene)	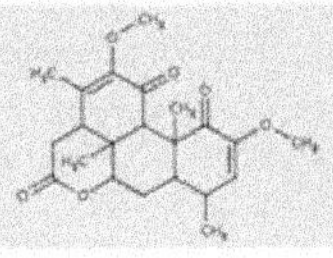	Quassia amara L / Simaroubaceae	Antimalarial

Table 2. List of some of the Terpenoids and their medicinal values.

Chemistry of Iridoids.

Iridoids are monoterpenoids based on a cyclopentan-[C]-pyran skeleton which may consist of ten, nine, or rarely eight carbon atoms in which C11 is more frequently missing than C10. Oxidative cleavage at 7, 8 bond of the cyclopentane moiety affords the so called secoiridoids. The stereo chemical configurations at C5 and C9 leading to cis fused rings are common to all iridoids containing the basic carbocyclic- or secoskeleton in non-rearranged form [9-14].

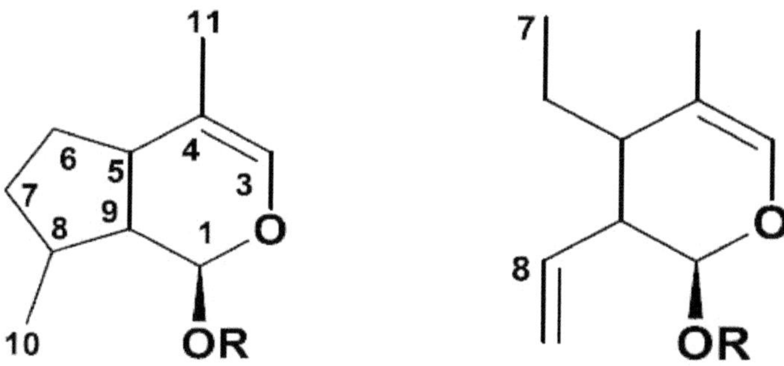

Fig: 4. Numbering system for iridoid and seco-iridoid compounds-R=H or glucose

Classification of Iridoids:

Iridoid can be classified as in different groups according to the basic carbon skeleton of the aglycone it is explained illustratively given below in **Fig. 1.15**

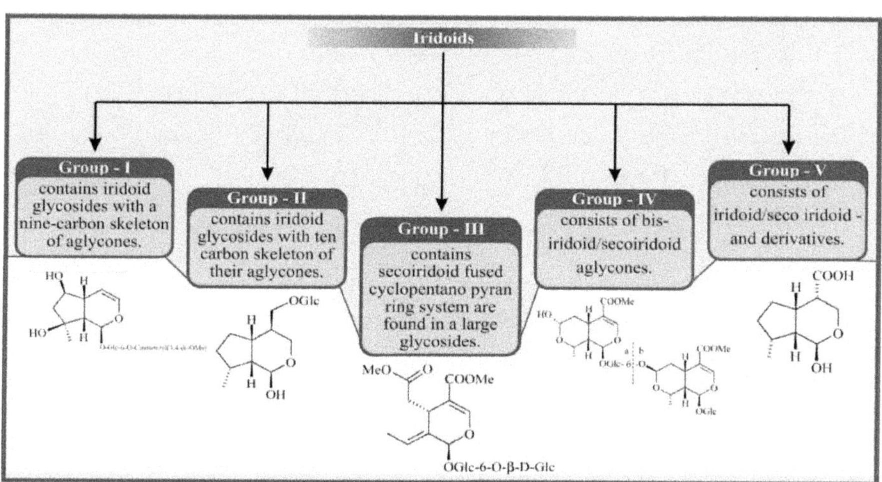

Fig: 5.Classification of Iridoids

Biogenesis of Iridoids:

The biosynthesis of iridoid can be divided into definite steps: 1. The iridoid ring scaffold is synthesized, in plants, by the enzyme synthase. In contrast with other monoterpene cyclases .

2. Iridoid synthase uses 10-oxogeranial as a substrate.

3. The enzyme uses a two-step mechanism, with an initial NADPH-dependent reduction step followed by a cyclization step that occurs through Iridane skeleton.

4. Iridane skeleton involve a double Michael-type addition or Diels alder cycloaddition of geranyl pyrophosphate to yield iridodial. Biogenesis of iridoids in Thunbergia species is given illustratively in **Figure 1.3.**

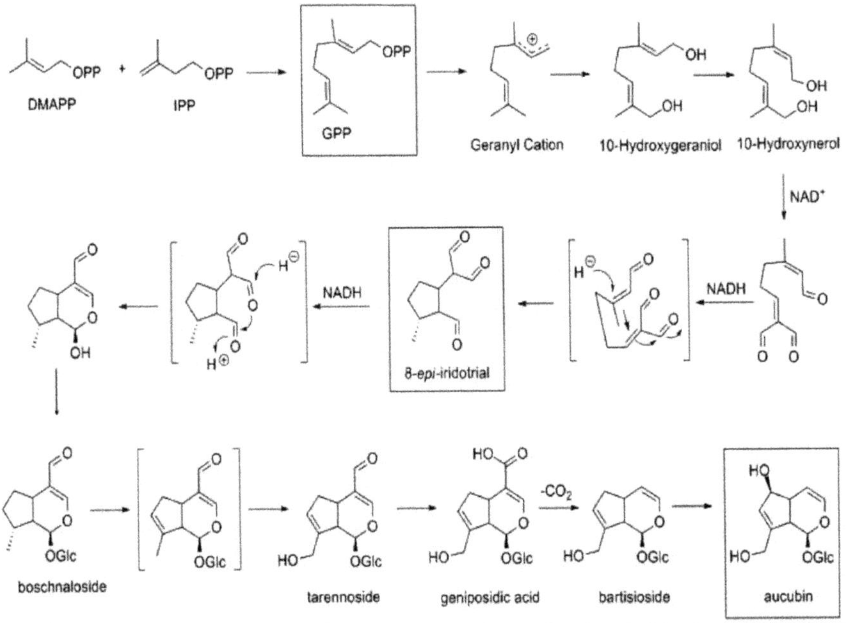

Fig: 1.6. Biogenesis of iridoids in Thunbergia species.

S.No	Iridoid / Seco-iridoid	Plant origin	Bio activity
1	Excelside B	*Faxinus excelsior*	Antidiabetic
2	Swertiamarin	*Enicostemma axillare*	Antinociceptive
3	Buddlejoside B	*Buddleja crispa*	Antihyperglycimic
4	Catalpol	*Rahmannia glutinosa*	Anti protazoal
5	6'-O-acetyl geniposide	*Garenia jasminoides*	Neuroprotective
6	Scandoside & perulosidic acid	*Morinda citrifolia*	Melanogenesis inhibitory activity
7	Rupesins C & D	*Partinia ruspestris*	Antibacterial
8	6-β-hydroxy-7-epigardoside methyl ester	*Alibertia edulis*	Antifungal
9	Prismatomerin	*Prismatomeris tetrandra*	Antitumor
10	6-O-Caffeoylharpagide	*Scrophularia ningpoensis*	Anticardiac
11	Genipin-1-O-α-L-rhamnopyranosyl (1-6)-β-D-glucopyranoside	*Adina polycephala*	Anti-coagulant
12	Picroside	*Neopicrorhiza scrophulariiflora*	Hepatoprotective

Table 3. List of some the iridoid / secoiridoids and their bioactivity.

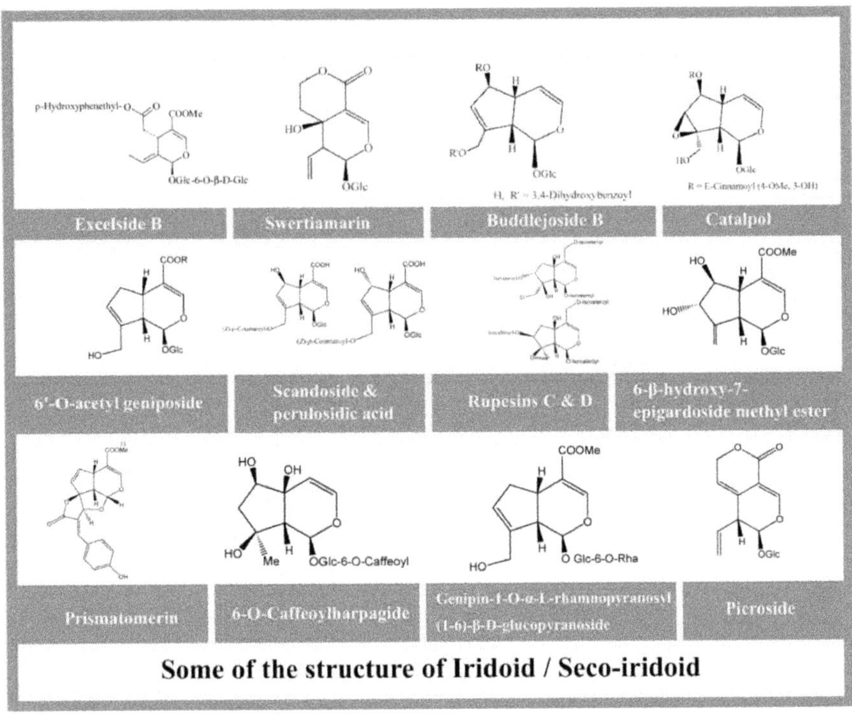

Fig.7. Some of Bio-active Structure of Iridoid/Seco-iridoid

Chemistry of Flavonoids

Flavonoids are a group of polyphenolic compounds, diverse in chemical structure and characteristics, found ubiquitously in plants. Flavonoids occur in a variety of structural forms. All contain fifteen carbon atoms in their parent nucleus and share the common structural features of two phenyl rings linked by a three carbon chain, i.e. biphenyl propane derivatives.

The compounds belonging to this class and possessing a 1, 3- diphenyl propane skeleton are regarded as chalconoids. The three carbon chain may be formed into a three, five or six membered ring through all oxygen on one of the phenyl rings generating a tricyclic system. The tricycles ring compounds possessing a five membered hetero cyclic ring referred to as auronoids, where those possessing a six membered heterocyclic ring are designated flavonoids and flavanoids. Similarly tricyclic compounds derived from 1, 2- biphenyl propane system are designated as isoflavonoids,

3-phenyl coumarins and pterocarponoids whereas those derived from 1, 1-diphenyl propane are called neoflavonoids. In tricyclic compounds of the flavonoid, auronoid and isoflavonoid types, rings are labeled A, B, C and the individual carbon atoms one referred to by numerals for the A- and C- rings and "primed" numerals for the B-ring [15-18].

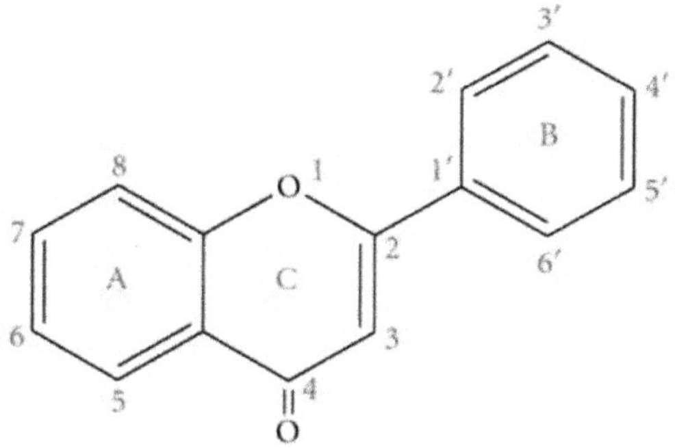

Fig: 8. Numbering system for basic skeleton of flavonoids compounds.

Naturally occurring polypheonls have two alternative modes of sugar linkage, viz., O-glycosylation or C – glycosylated compounds is that a direct carbon to carbon bond links the sugar portion of the molecule to the aglycone. Or non-sugar moiety leading to a single stable carbon frame work. Illustrative of this type are Vitexin and Orientin which contrast, with the more common O – glycosides having sugar residues attached to phenolic oxygen by C – O – C hemi acetal linkage. Glucose is the C – linked sugar in a vast majority of the C – glycosides. α-L Rhamnose and β-D Xylose form the sugar moiety in the remaining examples.

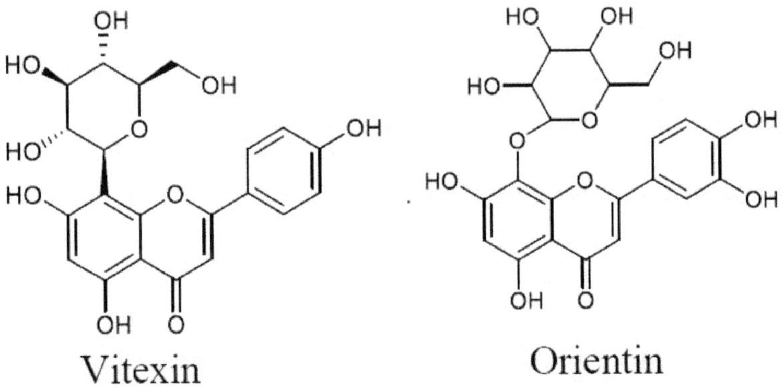

Vitexin

Orientin

Fig.9. Structure of Vitexin and Orientin

Classification of Flavonoids:

Various sub groups of flavonoids are classified as the substitution patterns of ring C. Both the oxidation state of heterocyclic ring and the position of ring B are important in the classification. Examples and sources as the 6 major subgroups are given below.

Name of the Flavonoids	Examples	
(1) Isoflavones	Daidzein	Glycitein
(2) Flavonols	Catechin	Epigallocatechin
(3) Flavones	Chrysin	Apigenin
(4) Flavanols	Kaempferol	Quercetin
(5) Flavanones	Naringin	
(6) Anthocyanidins	Cynadin	Malvidin

Table 4. Classification of Flavonoids.

Phenolic acids

Phenolic acids constitute also an important class of phenolic compounds with bioactive functions, usually found in plant and food products. Phenolic acids can be divided in two subgroups according to their structure: the hydroxybenzoic and the hydroxycinnamic acids. The most commonly found hydroxybenzoic acids include gallic, p-hydroxybenzoic, protocatechuic, vanillic and syringic acids, while among the hydroxycinnamic acids, caffeic, ferulic, p-coumaric and sinapic acids can be pointed out.

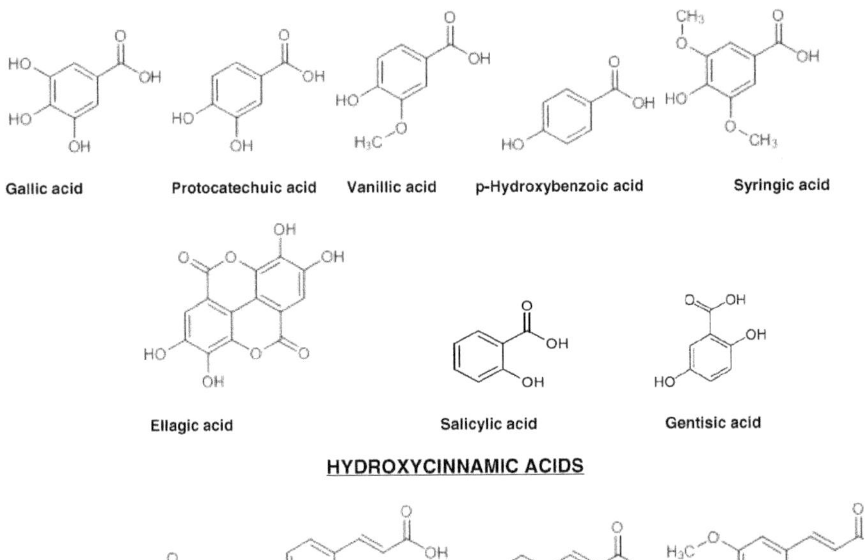

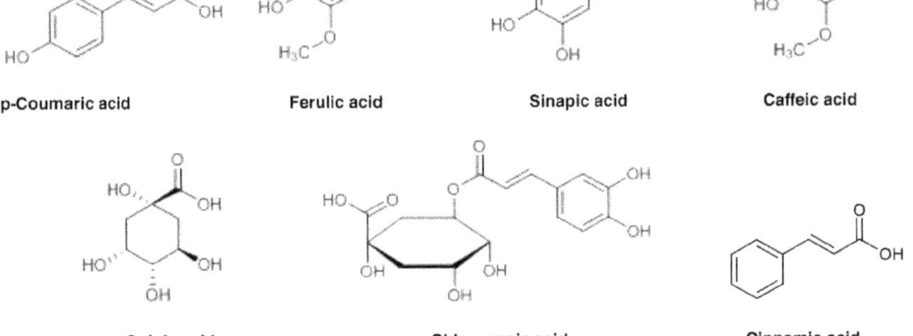

Fig.10. Some of the Structures of Phenolic Acids

Biogensis of Flavonoids and phenolic acids:

Flavonoid and phenolic acids were synthesized by the phenylpropanoid metabolic pathway in which the amino acid phenylalanine is used to produce 4-coumaroyl-CoA .This can be combined with malonyl-CoA to yield the true backbone of flavonoids, a group of compounds called chalcones, which contain two phenyl rings. Conjugate ring-closure of chalcones results in the familiar form of flavonoids, the three-ringed structure of a flavone. The metabolic pathway continues through a series of enzymatic modifications to yield flavanones → dihydroflavonols → anthocyanins. Along this pathway, many products can be formed, including the flavonols, flavan-3-ols, proanthocyanidins (tannins) and a host of other various polyphenolics. Biogenesis of flavonoids and phenolic acids is given illustratively in **Figure 1.6.**

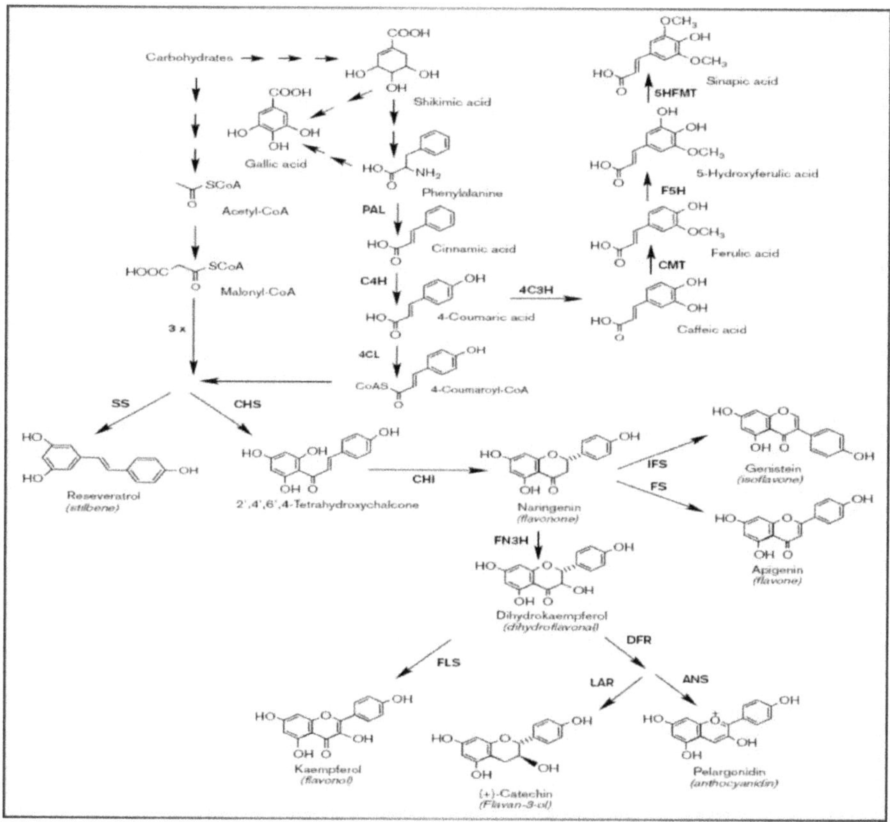

Fig: 11. Biogenesis of phenolic acids and flavonoids from genus Thunbergiea

S.No	Name of the Flavanoids	Source	Bio activity
1	Luteolin	*Terminalia chebula*	Antioxidant activity
2	Myricetin	Red wine	Pancreatic cancer
3	Quercetin	Apples	Cancer
4	Kaempferol	Grapefruit	Reduced risk of heart disease
5	Apigenin	Parsley, celery and chamomile tea	Treatment of neurological diseases
6	Malvidin	*Anagallis monelli*	Natural Colorants for Food and Nutraceutical
7	Rutin	*Carpobrotus edulis*	Anti-inflammatory
8	Naringenin	Peals of Oranges and tomatoes	Reduce hepatitis C virus
9	Hesperidin	Citrus fruits	Reduced cholesterol and blood pressure
10	Rhamnetin	Cloves	Inhibits human prostate cancer cell
11	Isorhamnetin	*Tagetes lucida*	Induces apoptosis
12	Eriodictyol	*Eriodictyon californicum*	Scavenged ROS
13	Genistein	Soy products	Prevention of breast and prostate cancer
14	Glycitein	Soy food products	Phytoestrogen with weak estrogenic activity
15	Catechin	*Acacia catechu*	Inhibits intestinal tumor
16	Patulitrin	Tagetes erecta (L.)	Wound Healing
17	Pedalitin	*Pedaliium murex*	Xanthine oxidase inhibitor
18	Galangin	*Helichrysum aureonitens*	Anti viral
19	Epicatichin	Cocoa, tea and grapes	Improves heart health
20	Silibinin	*Silybum marianum*	Anti-cancer effects against human prostate adenocarcinoma cells
21	Delphindin	Bilberry	Alzheimer's disease
22	Chrycin	*Passiflora caerulea*	Anti-inflammatory effects
23	Tangeritin	Citrus peels	Anticancer
24	Quercetagetin	*Eriocaulon*	Anti-inflammatory
25	Taxifolin	*Larix sibirica*	To inhibit the ovarian cancer cell growth
26	Pinobanksin	Sun flower honey	Inhibits peroxidation
27	Vitexin	Passion flower	Anti oxidant
28	Alpinumisoflavone	*Millettia thonningii*	antischistosomal

Table 5. List of some of the Flavonoids and their bioactivity.

Chemistry of Quinone.

Quinones are a large class of organic compounds such as benzene or naphthalene by conversion of an even number of –CH= groups into –C (=O) – groups with any necessary rearrangement of double bonds, resulting in a fully conjugated cyclic dione structural compounds. It is endowed with rich and fascinating chemistry. They are generally hydroxylated with phenolic properties and combined form of sugar as glucose some times dimeric forms. Quinones molecules a lipid-soluble character and mainly as electron and proton carriers in photosynthetic and respiratory electron transport chains, such as antioxidant function.

Classification and bio-activity of Quinones:

The member of the classes cyclohexadienedione, often called simply quinone, thus the name of the simple quinones, other important classes of quinones and their bio activity were given illustratively in **Table 1.6.**

S.No	Name of the Quinones	Example	Structure	Plant orgin	Bio activity
1.	Napthaquinones	Alkannin	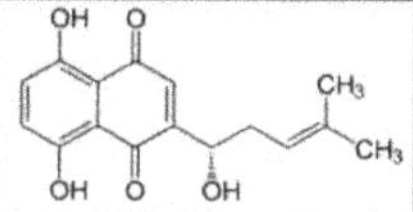 OH O CH$_3$ CH$_3$ OH O OH	*Alkanna tinctoria*	Antimalarial and anticoagulant
2.	Anthroquinones	Aloe - emodin	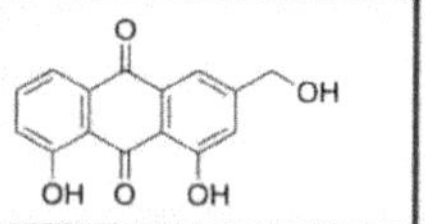 O OH OH O OH	*Aloe vera*	Antibiotic and antitumor
3.	Isoprenoid quinones	Menaquinone	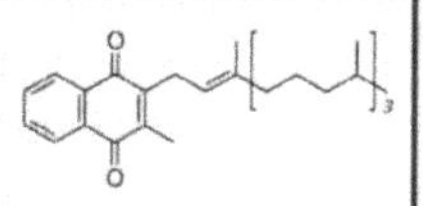 O O 3	green leafy vegetables	Herbicidal activity
4.	1, 4 - benzoquinone	Embelin	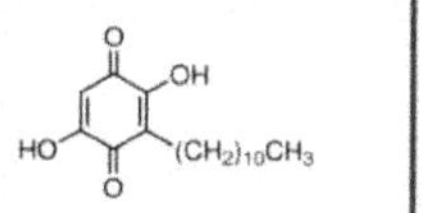 O OH HO (CH$_2$)$_{10}$CH$_3$ O	*Embelia schimperi*	Antimicrobial

Table 6. Classification and their bioactivity of Quinones.

Biogenesis of Quinone:

Quinone biosynthesis shows a much diversified picture. It often differs in higher plants. Most of the higher quinones arise by the polyketide pathway or shikimic acid or by mixed pathways. The three carbon atoms originate from three central carbons in glutamic acid or 2-keto-glutaric acid which react with iso-chorismate. The reaction is mediated by thiamine pyrophosphate. The shikimic acid have shown that the ring junction occur at carbon 1 and 2. Biogenesis of Quinones is given illustratively in **Figure 12.**

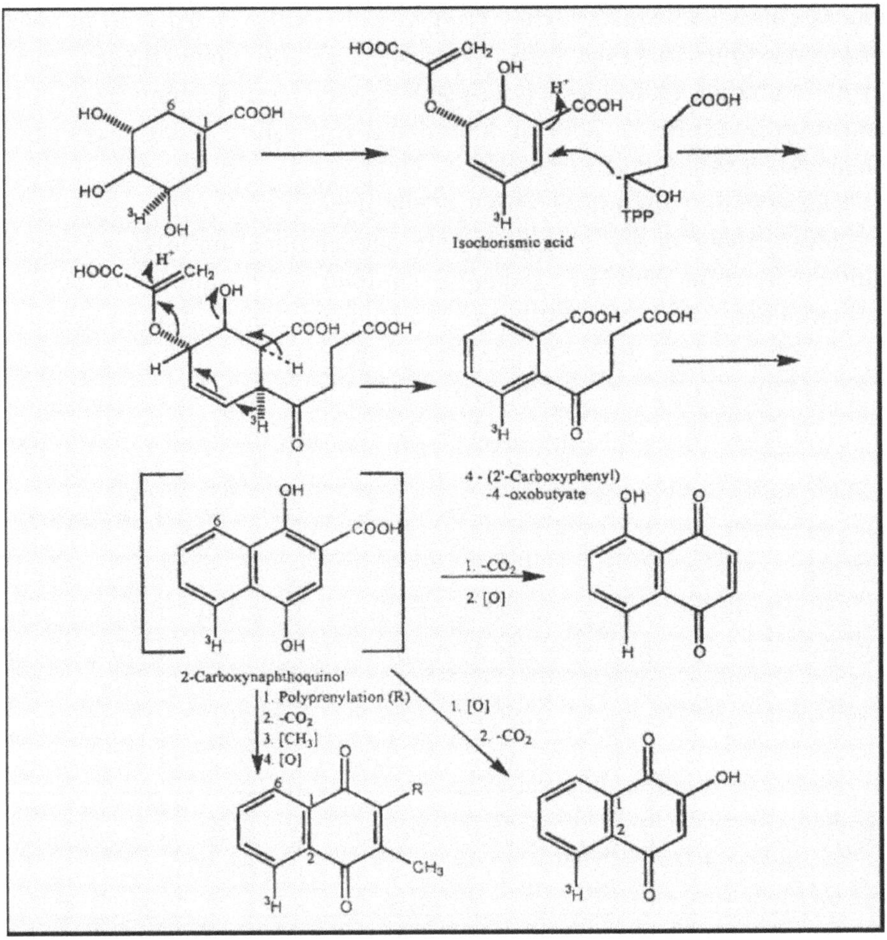

Fig.12. Biogenesis of Quinones

Chemistry of Coumarin

Coumarin is a naturally occurring benzo-a-pyrone (lactone type) compound and can be found in a large number of plants from different families including, tonka beans, woodruff, lavender oil, cassia (bark oil of common cinnamon source) and melilot (sweet clover). The chemistry of coumarins has centered on performing reactions at the activated C-3, 4-double bond of α, β-unsaturated lactone. Based on this heterocyclic systems have been built. Most of these coumarins are mono- or deoxygenated on the aromatic ring [19-23].

Classification of Coumarins:

Coumarins are classified based on the substitution in benzene and pyrone rings it is explained by illustratively in **Table 1.9.**

S.No	Type of coumarin	General chemical structure	Examples
1.	Simple coumarins	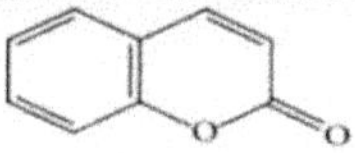	Coumarin
2.	Furano coumarins	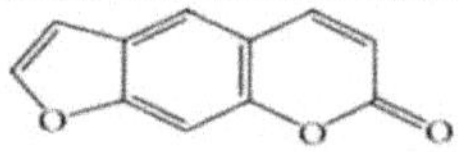	Methoxsalen
3.	Dihydrofurano coumarins	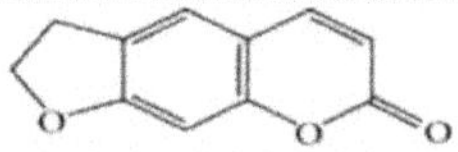	Marmesin
4.	Pyrano coumarins -Linear type	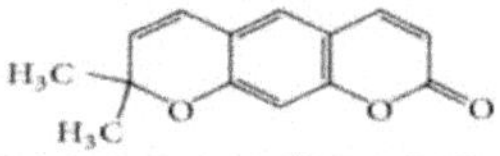 H_3C, H_3C	Agasyllin
5.	Pyrano coumarins -Angular type	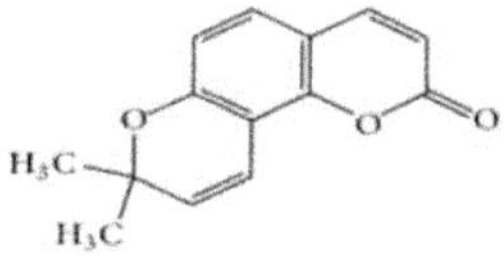 H_3C, H_3C	Dihydrocalanolide A and B
6.	Phenyl coumarins	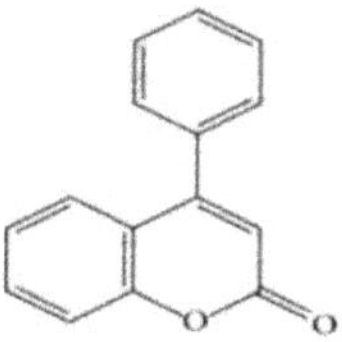	Disparpropylinol
7.	Bicoumarins	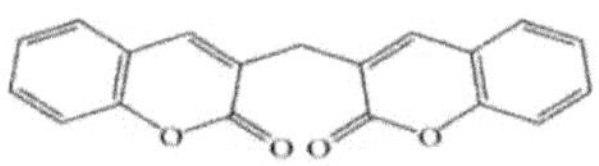	Dicoumarol

Table 7. Classification of Coumarin.

Biogenesis of Coumarins:

The coumarin structure is derived from cinnamic acid via ortho-hydroxylation trans-cis isomerization of the side chain double bond and lactonisation. The trans form is stable and could not cyclize, therefore, there should be isomerization of some sort and the enzyme isomerase is implicated. Biogenesis of coumarins is illustratated in given below **Figure 1.9.**

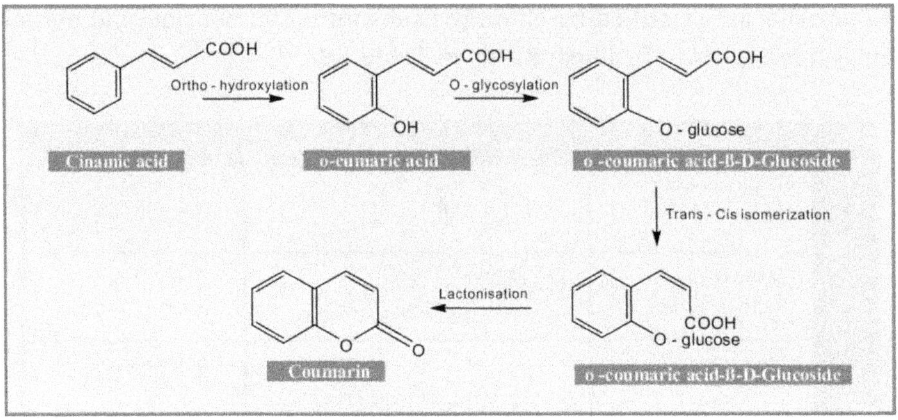

Fig 18. Biogenesis of coumarins.

S.No	Name of the Coumarin	Structure	Source	Bioactivity
1.	Esculetin	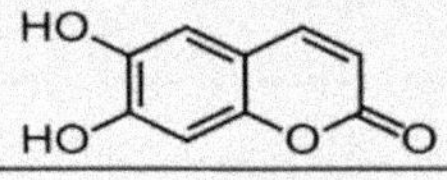	Chicory	Antiadipogenic
2.	Scopoletin	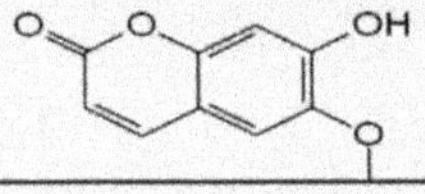	*Scopolia carniolica*	Nicotinic agonist property
3.	Fraxin	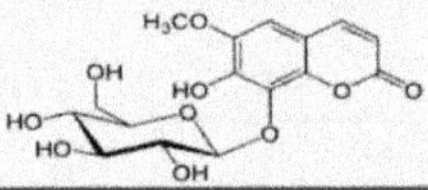	*Actinidia chinensis*	Antioxidant
4.	Umbelliferone	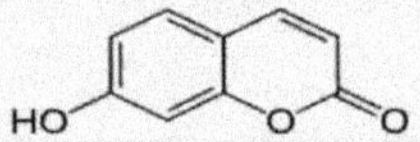	Carrot	Antitubercula
5.	Imperatorin	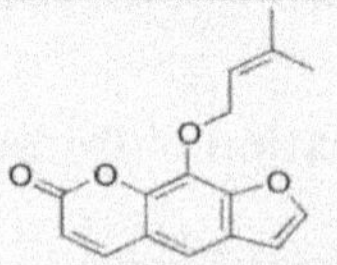	*Zanthoxylum americanum*	Antiviral
6.	Psoralen	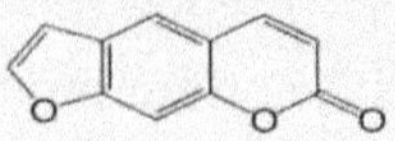	*Psoralea corylifolia*	Anti-TB

Table 8. List of some of the Coumarin and their bioactivity.

Chemistry of Lignans.

Lignans, by convention, are a group of natural products that are formed by linking two phenylpropanoid units (C6C3 units) by oxidative coupling. Most importantly, in a lignan, two (C6C3 units) are bound through the central carbon of their side chains, i.e. the 8 and 8' positions. The occurrence of C6C3-dimers, linked at sites other than the 8–8' positions, is also known and these compounds have been termed neolignans [24-35].

Classification of Lignans:

Conventional lignan-Two groups (lignan and neolignan) of compounds have close structural as well as biosynthetic relationships, they are often associated together and incorporated under the general term "Conventional lignan or True lignan".

Non-conventional lignan- Two C6C3 units linked together but have additional structural features to place them also under the category of coumarins, flavonoids, stilbenes, or xanthones. The diverse structural categorization of true lignans and of a few neolignans and non-conventional lignans are represented below illustratively in **Table 9.**

Name of the Lignans	*Structural patterns*
(1) Conventional *lignans and neolignans*	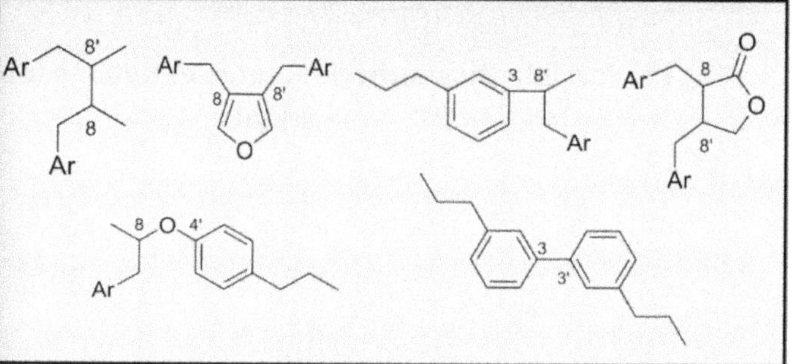 Ar, 8', 8, Ar; Ar, Ar, 8, 8', O; 3, 8', Ar; Ar, 8, O, O, 8', Ar; 8, O, 4', Ar; 3, 3'
(2) Non Conventional *Coumarino, flavono and stilbino lignan*	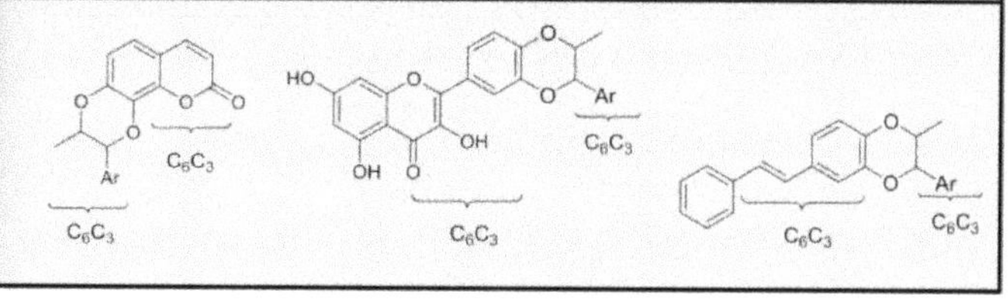 O, O, O, O, Ar, C_6C_3, C_6C_3; HO, O, O, O, Ar, OH, OH, O, C_6C_3, C_6C_3; O, O, Ar, C_6C_3, C_6C_3

Table 9. Classification of Lignans

Biogenesis of Lignans:

Oxidation of coniferyl alcohol to different mesomeric radicals, whose coupling could yield Quinone methides intermediates These primary coupling products were supposed to be able to add water, coniferyl alcohol, or even another molecule of the same kind to yield products which, on further oxidation or polymerization, could give polymeric substances like lignin's. Birch's cinnamyl pyrophosphate derivative can afford radicals located at the β-carbon in two ways. Either by direct oxidation. Both radicals and are highly stabilized and it becomes clear why their coupling products, the neolignans. Biogenesis of lignans and neolignan is explained below in figure 1.10 and figure 1.11.

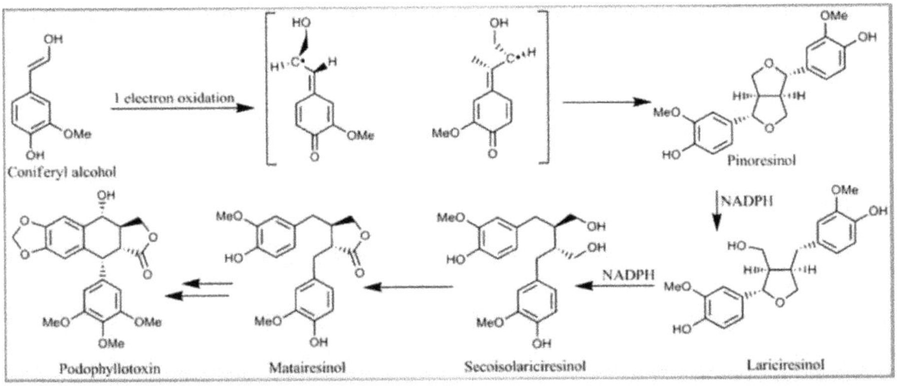

Fig 14. Possible Biosynthetic Routes to lignans found in Lauraceous plants.

Fig: 15. Possible Biosynthetic Routes to Neolignans found in genus Alseodaphne.

S.No.	Name of the lignan	Plant orgin	Bio activity
1	Podophyllotoxins	*Podophyllum sp*	Inhibit topoisomerase II
2	Episteganangin	*Steganotaenia araliacea*	Cytotoxic
3	(-)-arctigenin	*Forsythia intermedia*	Anti - HIV
4	Anolignan A	*Anogeissus acuminata var. lanceolata*	Inhibition of HIV-1 RT
5	Termilignan	*Terminalia bellerica*	Anti-HIV-1, assay using MT-4 cells
6	Asarinin	*Asiasarum heterotropoides var. mandshuricum*	Inhibited Epstein-Barr virus (EBV)
7	Dihydrodiisoeugenol	*Myristica fragrans*	Antibacterial
8	Nyasol	*Asparagus africanus*	Antiprotozoal agent
9	Phyllanthin	*Phyllanthus niruri*	Endothelin antagonism
10	Sesamin	*Sesamum indicum*	Effects on Metabolism and Cholesterol Level
11	Wuweizisu B	*Schisandra chinensis*	Antioxidant
12	Silybin	*Silybum marianum*	Hepatoprotective

Table 10. List of some of the Lignans and their bioactivity

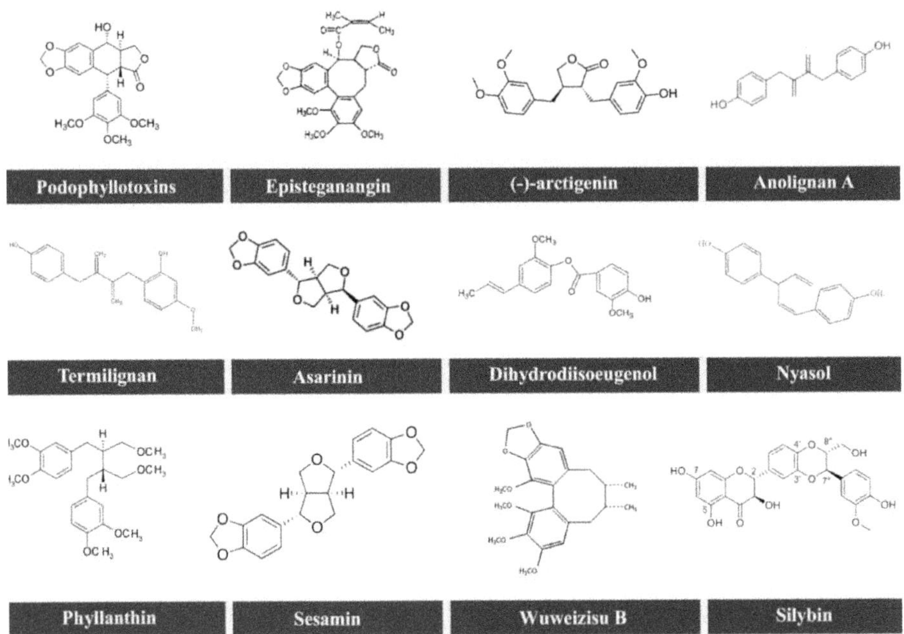

Fig 16. Structure of Lignans and their bioactivity

Chemistry of alkaloids

Alkaloids means Alkali likes. The Pharmacist W.Meissner proposed the term Alkaloids in 1819. According to him "Alkaloids (alkali = base, oid=like sub) are basic nitrogenous compound of plant origin which have complex molecular structure and many pharmacological activity.

"According to Landenberg "Alkaloids are defined as natural plant compounds that have a basic character and contain at least one nitrogen atom in a heterocyclic ring and having biological activities."

"According to characteristic features of alkaloids are basic nitrogenous plant origin, mostly optically active and possessing nitrogen hetero cycles as there structural units with physiological action. “According to Pelletier 1983 “an alkaloids is cyclic compounds containing nitrogen in negative of oxidation state. Which is of limited distribution in Living organisms[36-40].

Classification of Alkaloids:

1) Taxonomic based: According to their family e.g. Solanaceous, Papilionaceous, Lauraceous without reference their chemical type of alkaloids present and another according to genus

2) Pharmacological based: Their pharmacological activity or response. For example:

1. Analgesic alkaloids.
2. Cardio active alkaloids.
3. Hypotensive alkaloids etc. Do not have chemical similarity in their group.

3) Bio Synthetic based: According to this alkaloids are classified on the basis of the type precursors or building block compounds used by plants to synthesis the complex structure.

4) Chemical classification: This classification is universally adopted and depends on the fundamental ring structure. The above mentioned classification are explained by the structural pattern of alkaloids. The illustrations given below.

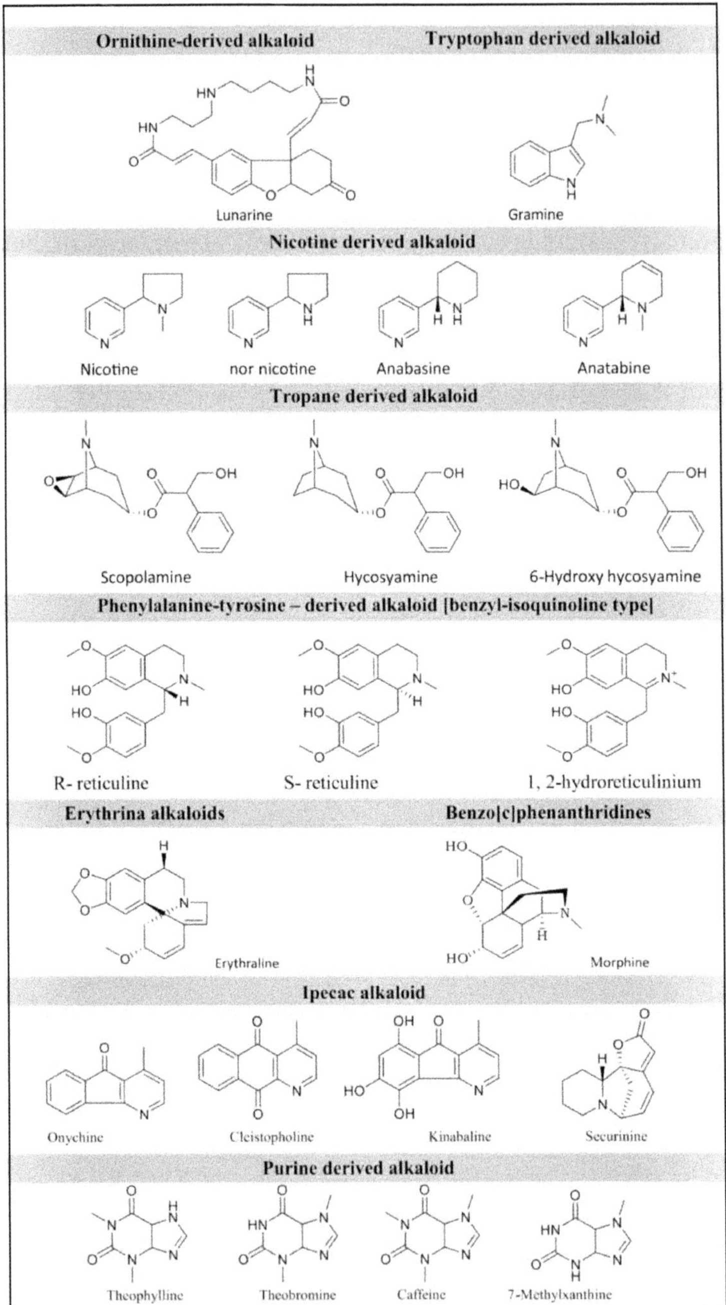

Fig 17. Structures of Alkaloid

Biogenesis of alkaloids:

Lauranceae species have been recognized for a long time as a source of alkaloids. Benzyl tetra hydroiso quinolines and aporphines are probably present in most of their members. The benzyl tetra hydroiso quinolines are biosynthetically the simplest of these alkaloidal types. They derive by a few well known steps from phenylalanine or tyrosine. Two mojor pathways are available for skeletal modifications of these primary alkaloids. Intramolecular oxidative coupling which leads via spirodienones (pro-aporphines) to aporphines, as well as intermolecular oxidative coupling which leads to bis-benzyl- tetrahydoisquinolines. Biogenesis of alkaloids is discussed illustratively in **Figure 1.6.**

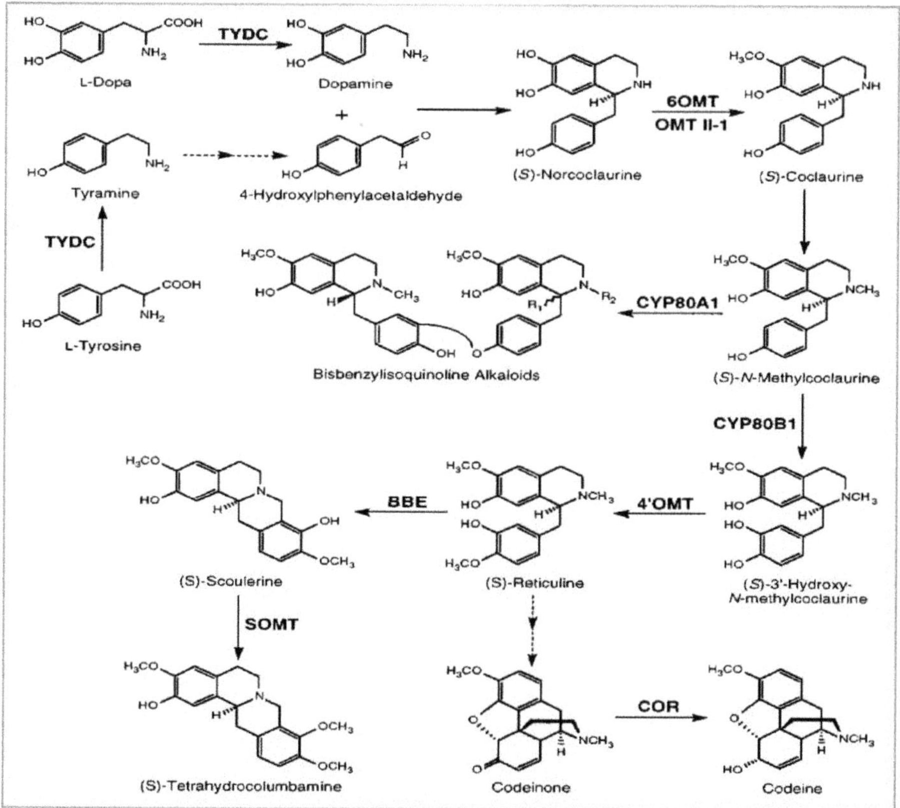

Fig: 18. Biogenesis of alkaloids from genus Alseodaphane.

S.No	Name of the Alkaloid	Plant orgin	Bioactivity
1	Cocaine	*Coca leaves*	CNS stimulant
2	Quinine	*Cinchona succirubra*	Antiarrhythmic, antimalarial
3	Nicotine	*Nicotiana tobacum*	Alzheimer
4	Lobeline	*Lobelia inflata*	Cholinergic agonist
5	Arecoline	*Areca catechu*	Parasympathomimetic
6	Pilocarpine	*Pilocarpus jaborandi*	Myosis of the eye
7	Neostigmine	*Physostigma vensum*	Irreversible chorine esterase inhibitor
8	Reserpine and Rescinnamine	*Rauwlfia serpentine*	Anti-hypertensive
9	Morphine	*Pappaver somniferum*	Analgesic
10	Atropine	*Atropa belladona*	Antidote to nerve gas poisoning
11	Caffeine	Coffee bean	CNS stimulant
12	Colchicine	*Colchicum autumnale*	Treatment of gout, fever, pericarditis, and Behest's disease
13	Emitine	*Cephalis Spp.*	Cure dysentery
14	Irenoteccan	*Mappia foitida* Miers	Lung cancer
15	Comptothescin	*Comptotheca acuminate*	Cervical cancer
16	Ajmalicine	*Mitragyna speciosa*	Antihypertensive drug used in the treatment of high blood pressure
17	Onychine	*Cleistopholis patens*	Anticandidal activity
18	Erythraline	*Erythrina crista-galli*	Treatment of inflammation diseases, suppressed nitric oxide (NO) production
19	Scopoline	*Datura species*	Used as a sedative
20	Reticuline	*Annona squamosa*	Possesses potent CNS depressing effects
21	Vindoline	*Catrantaus roseus*	Anti-tumor agents
22	Theophyline	*Cocoa beans*	Drug used in therapy for respiratory diseases such as COPDand asthma
23	Indican	*Indigofera plants*	Hartnup's disease
24	Catharanthine	*Catharanthus roseus*	Anticancer
25	DIBOA	*Hordeium vulgare*	Cyclic Hydroxamic Acid Inhibitors of Prostate Cancer
26	Galanthamine	*Galanthus caucasicus*	Is used for the treatment of mild to moderate Alzheimer's disease and various other memory impairments
27	7-Methyl Xanthine	Tea, chocolate	Phosphodiesterase inhibitors
28	Strictosidine	*Voacanga africana*	To exhibit potent cytotoxicity to the A549 cancer cell line
29	Kinabaline	*Meiogyne virgata*	Anti-microbial

Table: 11. List of some of the Alkaloids and their bioactivity.

Chemistry of Phytosterols.

Phytosterols or phytostanols are referred as plant sterols are common plant and vegetable constituents and are therefore normal constituents of the human diet. Sterols of plants are called phytosterols and sterols of animals are called zoo sterols. The most important zoo sterol are structurally related to cholesterol, but phyto sterols differ from cholesterol in the structure of the side chain. They are a large group of compounds that are found exclusively in plants and consist if a steroid skeleton with a hydroxyl group attached to the C-3 atom of the A-ring and an aliphatic side chain attached to the C-17 atom of the D-ring. Phytosterols have a double bond, typically between C-5 and C-6 of the sterol moiety, whereas this bond is saturated in phytostanols. Basic skeleton and numbering system of phytosterols given below in **Figure 19.**

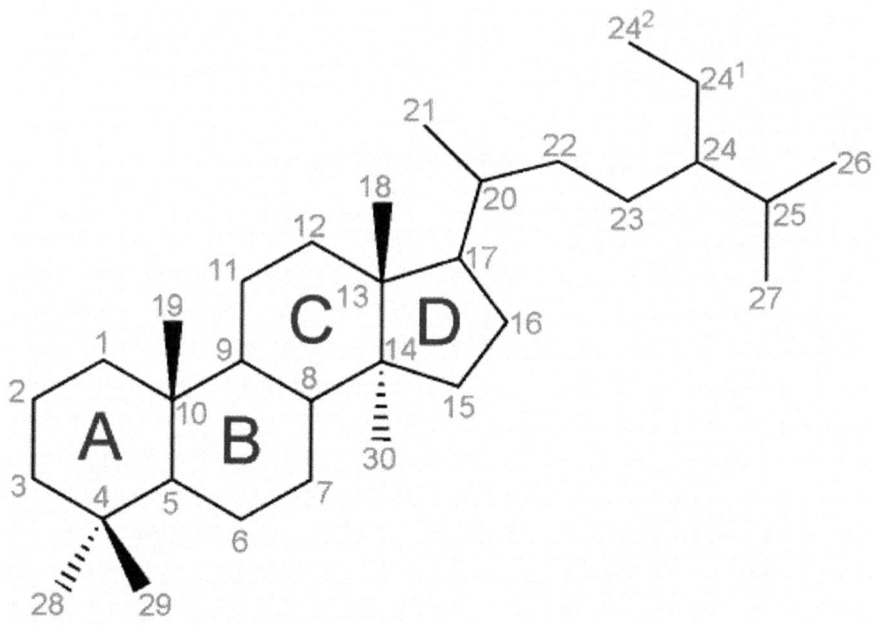

Fig: 19. Numbering system for basic skeleton of Phytosterols.

Classification of Phytosterols:

Chemical classification of phytosterols are a sub group of steroids with a hydroxyl group at the 3 position and a notable phytosterols diversified in structural side chain include here it can be classified as illustratively given

below in **Fig. 20**

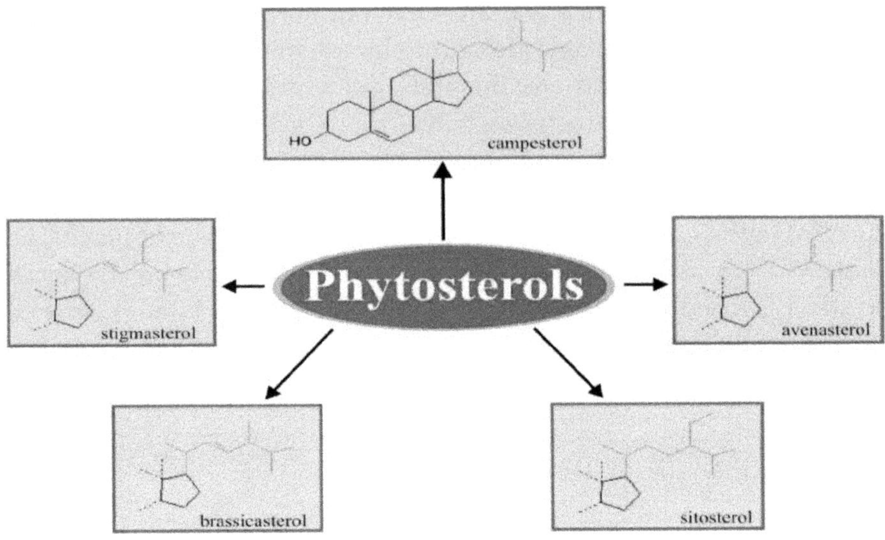

Fig: 20. Classification of Phytosterols

Biogenesis of Phytosterols: Tail-to-tail formation of squalene, a triterpene via malavonate pathway. Squalene, through a cyclization reaction with 2, 3-oxidosqualene as an intermediate forms cycloartenol. The double bond of cycloartenol is methylated by S-Adenosyl methionine (SAM) to give a carbocation that undergoes a hydride shift and loses a proton to yield a compound with a methylene side-chain. Both of these steps are catalyzed by sterol C-24 methyltransferase. Then catalyzed by sterol C-4 demethylase and loses a methyl group to produce cycloeucalenol. Subsequent to this, the cyclopropane ring is opened with cycloeucalenol cycloisomerase to form 24-Methelene lophenol. Then loses a methyl group and undergoes an allylic isomerization to form Campesterol. This step is catalyzed by sterol C-14 demethylase, sterol Δ14-reductase, and sterol Δ8-Δ7-isomerase. The last methyl group is removed by sterol. Biogenesis of phytosterols is illustratively given below in **Figure 21.**

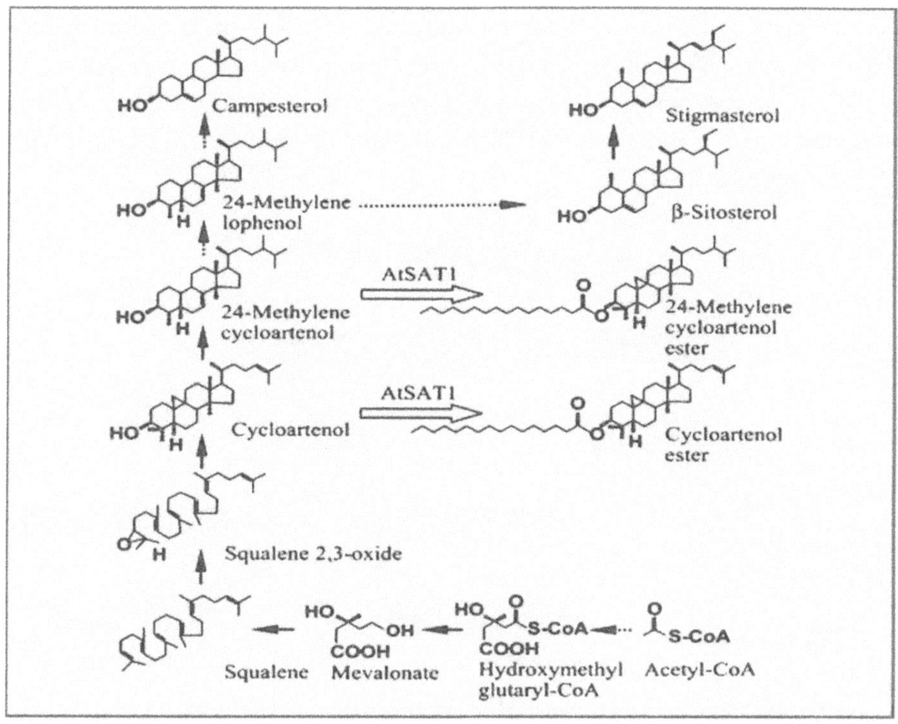

Fig: 21. Biogenesis of Phytosterols.

Bioactivity of Phytosterol:

Free or esterified forms of phytosterols are added to foods for their properties to reduce the absorption of cholesterol in the gut and thereby lower blood cholesterol levels. It is now generally accepted that sterols and stanols have the same cholesterol-lowering efficacy.

Chemistry of Saponin

Naturally occurring saponins are bio active glycoside of steroids, alkaloids, and triterpenoid compounds often referred to as a "natural detergent" because of their foamy texture. Saponins are in a diverse group to glycosides and are mainly of the triterpenoidal type, being the oleanolic acid and the hedagenin the main constituents [41-49].

Classification of Saponins:

Saponins are glycosidic compounds composed of a steroid (C-27) or triterpenoid (C-30) saponin nucleus can possess from one to three straight or branched sugar chains, most often composed of d-glucose, l-rhamnose, d-galactose, d-glucuronic acid, l-arabinose, d-xylose or d-fructose. The sugar chain can contain from one to several monosaccharide residues, and is usually attached at C-31. The aglycone can further classified as neutral and acidic saponin (Steroid or Triterpenoidal skeleton) it is given below illustratively in **Fig. 22.**

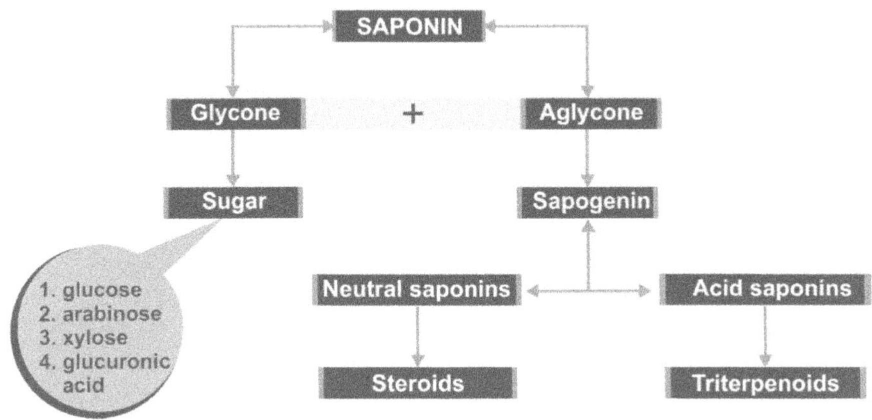

Fig:22. Classification of saponins

Biogenesis of Saponins:

Saponins are derivatives of steroids with spiroketal side chains, whereas acid saponins possess triterpenoid structures. The main pathway for biogenesis of sapogenins is similar. However, a branch occurs, probably after formation of triterpenoid hydrocarbon-squalene which leads to cyclic triterpenoids in one direction and spiroketal steroids in other direction. The bio production of squalene, cholesterol and various steroidal compounds including the aglycones is outlined and the biogenesis of Saponins is illustratively mentioned below in **Fig. 23.**

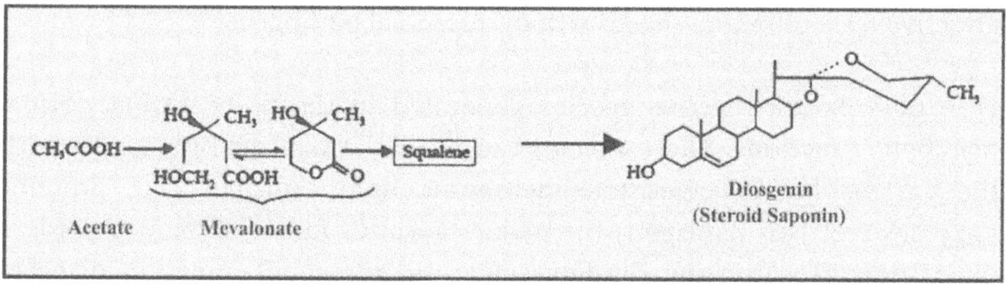

Fig: 23. Biogenesis of saponins

S.No	Name of the Saponins	Plant origin	Medicinal values
1	Aescin	*Aesculus hippocastanum*	Vasoconstrictor and vasoprotective
2	Glycyrrhizin	licorice root	Treatment of gastric ulcers
3	Saikosaponin A	*Bupleurum falcatum L.*	Anti-cancer
4	Senegin II	*Polygala senega*	Antidiabetic
5	Astragaloside III	*Astragalus membranaceus*	Regulators of CD45 protein tyrosine phosphatase
6	Bacosides A	*Bacopa monnieri*	Enhanced memory

Table:12. List of some the Saponins and their bioactivity.

ANTI-MICROBIAL AND ANTIOXIDANTS NATURAL PRODUCTS5

Antibiotics, antiseptics and disinfectants and are used in different ways to combat microbial growth. Antiseptics are used on living tissue to remove pathogens. Disinfectants are similar in use but are used on inanimate objects. Laboratories, world-wide thousands of phytochemicals which have inhibitory effects on all types of microorganisms in vitro. Agar well diffusion method is an in vitro techniques in which standard zones of inhibition have been determined for susceptible and resistant values. This technique is commonly used for determination of Minimum Inhibitory Concentration in solid media. Phytochemical of different concentration were placed on the surface into agar plate seeded with the test bacterial strain. Diffusion from these source into agarose medium leads to inhibition of bacterial growth. Other than in vitro techniques most of these compounds shall be tried to animals and human beings to determine their effectiveness inhibiting the growth of microbial pathogens[50-52].

Free radicals are reactive species generated in the body during normal metabolic functions. These species cause cellular damage by reacting with the various biomolecules like membrane lipids, nucleic acid, proteins enzymes etc. This damage is the major causative factor of many disorders like Cancer, Hepatopathy, Cardiovascular disorders, inflammation, diabetes mellitus, renal failure and brain dysfunction.

Body has itself antioxidant system which reacts with reactive species and neutralizes them. This natural antioxidant system includes enzymes like catalase, superoxide dismutase and glutathione. They protect the body from free radical species and prevent oxidative stress. Synthetic antioxidant like butylated hydroxyl toluene and butylated hydroxyl anisole are carcinogenic in nature. So, there arises a need for natural antioxidant. Accumulated evidence suggests that Reactive Oxygen Species can be scavenged through chemoprevention utilizing natural antioxidant compounds present in foods and medicinal plants. Antioxidant-based drug formulations are used for the prevention and treatment of complex diseases like atherosclerosis, stroke, diabetes, Alzheimer's disease and cancer. Some of in-vitro assay followed the anti-oxidant activity studies of medicinal plant extracts such as DPPH, ABTS, supper oxide scavenging assays etc.

ANTI-INFLAMATORY AND ANALGESICS NATURAL PRODUCTS56-
Pain, heat, redness, and swelling (dolor, calor, rubor, and tumor) are the various manifestations of the inflammatory processes. Inflammation is the response to injury of cells and body tissues through different factors such as infections, chemicals, thermal and mechanical injuries. Prostaglandins act as the short-lived localized hormones that can be released by any cell of the body when tissue get injured. They can induce fever, inflammation and pain at once they are present in the intercellular space.

The research into the medicinal plants which have been used in folk medicines pain relivers and anti-inflammatory agents, focusses on pinning down the newer drugs. Thus, many of these natural compounds also work by inhibiting the inflammatory pathways in a similar manner as Non-Steroid Anti-inflammatory Drugs (NSAIDS). In addition to the COX pathway, many natural compounds act to inhibit nuclear factor-kB (NF-kB) inflammatory pathways. The laboratory evolution of analgesics was formerly to studies on experimental pain in animal models by physical and chemical influences. Some of the important pain reliever /anti-inflammatory agents isolated from plant origin given below in **Table.13.**

S.No	Anti-inflammatory / pain reliever	Plant origin
1.	Capsaicin	*Capsicum annum*
2.	Trans - Resveratrol	*Polygonum cuspidatum / Red wine*
3.	*Frankincense*	*Boswellia serrataresin*
4.	Epigallocatechin	Green Tea
5.	Curcumin	Turmeric
6.	Morphine	*Papaver somniferum*
7.	Pycnogenol	Maritime pine bark

Table 13. List of some of the anti-inflammatory and pain reliever agents from plant sources

ANTI-CANCER NATURAL PRODUCTS53-55

In recent times, there has been a lot of progress in cellular and molecular biology. It has helped us in understanding different mechanisms of this cancerous diseases. More and more anticancer drugs and vaccines have been developed. Natural products have contributed significantly to the development of anticancer drugs. According to a recent review, among the 79 Food and Drug Administration (FDA) approved anticancer drugs and vaccines during the year 1983-2002, 9 of them were the natural products and 21 of them were derivatives of the natural product. Also among the 39 synthetic anticancer drugs, 13 of them were based on a pharmacophore originated from natural compounds [53-55].

Currently, there are a large number of bioassay systems in the area of anticancer drugs. They are divided into two groups- cellular assays and cell-free assays. Cellular assays utilize intact cells (yeast cells, mammalian cells, etc.). The cell-free assays utilize isolated systems (enzymes, DNA fragments, etc.) for bioactivity study. These cell-free assays are usually mechanism-based, with a key enzyme or other biomolecule as the target.

Cytotoxicity assays are very commonly used in cellular assays. Since cytotoxicity is an activity that is consistent with anticancer activity, the major advantage of cytotoxicity assays is that all potential mechanisms of cellular proliferation can be monitored simultaneously. Thus, the search for new anti-cancer drugs in the past has been primarily focused on extracts showing cytotoxicity to one or two cell lines. Many have established methods such as Colony Formation method, Crystal Violet method, Tritium-Labeled Thymidine Uptake method, MTT, and WST methods, which are used for counting the number of live cells. Some of the important anticancer agents isolated from plant origin given below in Table.1.16.
Table 1.16. List of some the anti-cancer agents from plant sources.

ANTI-HIV NATURAL PRODUCTS
Human immuno deficiency virus (HIV) is a lenti virus (a member of the retrovirus family) that causes acquired immuno deficiency syndrome (AIDS), a condition in humans in which the immune system begins to fail, leading to life-threatening opportunistic infections. Once HIV enters the human body, its primary target is a subset of immune cells that contain a molecule called CD4. In particular, the virus attaches itself to CD4+T cells[56-62].

Three HIV enzymes are essential to the life cycle of the virus. HIV reverse transcriptase (RT) is crucial for viral replication. HIV protease processes viral polyproteins into functional enzymes and structural proteins, thereby facilitating maturation and infectivity of the virion particles. Without effective HIV PR, HIV remains uninfectious because its work in HIV is to create mature protein components by synthesizing poly protein. HIV-integrase mediate are HIV integration into the host chromosome. The chemotherapeutic strategies have therefore been focused on the development of inhibitors of these retroviral enzymes.

A schematic structure of a HIV-1 protease is given in above. The monomers are shown in green and cyan, the Asp-25 and Asp-25′ residues are shown in red, and Ile50 and Ile50′ residues linked to a water molecule are shown in purple. A number of researchers have authored excellent treatises reviewing the status of development of HIV RT inhibitors and HIV protease inhibitors. Diminished drug effectiveness as the virus develops resistance to current drugs. Therefore, novel compounds with unique modes of actions will be continually needed.

S.No	Anti-inflammatory / pain reliever	Plant origin
1.	Capsaicin	*Capsicum annum*
2.	Trans - Resveratrol	*Polygonum cuspidatum / Red wine*
3.	*Frankincense*	*Boswellia serrataresin*
4.	Epigallocatechin	Green Tea
5.	Curcumin	Turmeric
6.	Morphine	*Papaver somniferum*
7.	Pycnogenol	Maritime pine bark

Table 13. List of anti- HIV Natural Products.

Evaluation of in-silico methodologies and phytochemical data sources
Drug design is an important tool in the field of medicinal chemistry where new compounds are synthesized or isolated from plant origin by molecular or chemical manipulation of the lead moiety in order to produce highly active compounds with minimum steric effect. New drug discovery is considered broadly in terms of two kinds of investigational activities such as exploration and exploitation. Nowadays, the use of computers to predict the binding of libraries of small molecules to known target structures is an increasingly important component of the drug discovery process[63-64].

The computing resources considered included the various databases currently available and the software that has been or might be used in analyses of these data. The various different kinds of databases identified as relevant included those holding ethno botanical and/or chemical and/or pharmacological and/or toxicological data on the herbs, as well as those that hold data on known or potential molecular targets for the herbal constituents. The software tools considered as relevant included programs that provide for

1. Virtual screening of natural product libraries and chemical libraries,
2. Pattern recognition,
3. Bioinformatics studies relating to herbal data base and
4. The various data visualization and statistical analysis packages for proteomics / genomics / metabolomics studies

In-silico studies were defined as those involving virtual screening and/or cheminformatics, but more widely would also include those involving bioinformatics and the various different types of 'omics' studies. The view was universally held that any such studies could not be fruitfully performed by non-specialists – even though the software tools were often easily accessed and easily used by those unfamiliar with computational chemistry. It was unanimously accepted that the performance of in-silico studies in Natural product research necessitated close interaction between computational Chemists and Herbal Medicine experimentalists. Such interaction is common in the cross-disciplinary areas of molecular pharmacology and structural biology, and in-silico medicinal research would thus present no exception.

Entry	Compound	Plant origin(Family)	Chemical characteristics
1	Phorbol	*Excoecaria agallocha* (Euphorbiaceae)	Terpenoids
2	15-O-acetyl-3-O-butanoyl -5-O-propionyl-7-O-nicotinoylmyrsinol	*Euphorbia myrsinites*	Tetracyclic diterpene Tetraester
3	Dehydroandrographolide succinic acid monoester	*Andrographis paniculata* (Acanthaceae)	Diterpene lactone
4	Salaspermic acid	*Trypterygium wilfordii* (Celastraceae)	Pentacyclic triterpene
5	Inophyllum B	*Calophylium inophyllum* (Guttiferae)	Coumarin derivative
6	7-Glucuronic acid, 5,6-dihydroxyflavone	*Scutellaria baicalensis* (Labiatae)	Flavone
7	1,5,8-Trihydroxy-3-methoxy-7-(5',7',3",4"-tetrahydroxy-6'-C-β-D-glucopyranosyl-4'-oxy-8'-flavyl)-xanthone	*Swertia franchetiana* (Gentianaceae)	Flavone-xanthone C-glucoside
8	Putranijivain A	*Phyllanthus emblica* (Euphorbiaceae)	Tannin
9	Verticillatol	*Litsea verticillata (Lauraceae)*	Terpenoid
10	Repandusinic acid	*Phyllanthus niruri* (Euphorbiaceae)	Tannin

Table 1.17. List of phytochemical databases in recent times.

CHAPTER TWO

REFERENCES

1. Harborne,J.B. *Phytochemical methods, Chapman and Hall, London*, 1973, 52.
2. Krishnaaswamy,N.R. *Chemistry of Natural Products*, University Press, 1999, x.
3. Castello, M.C., Phattak, A., Chandra, N. and Sharon,M. *Antimicrobial activity of crude extracts from plant parts and corresponding calli of Bixa orellana L.* Indian Journal of experimental biology. 2002, 40(12):1378-1381.

4. Ertuk, O., Kati H., Yayli, N. and Demirbag, Z. *Antimicrobial properties of Silene mutifida (Adams) Rohrb. Plant extract.* Turk J. Biol. 2006, 30(1):17-21.

5. Mohnnta, T.K., Patra, J.K., Rath, S.K., Pal, D.K. and Thatoi, H.N. *Evaluation of antimicrobial activity and phytochemical screening of oils and nuts of Semicarpus anacardium L.f. Sci.res. Essay*. 2007; 2 (11): 486-490.

6. Kumar, A.R., Subburathinam, K.M. and Prabaker,G.*Phytochemical screening of selected medicinal plants of Asclepiadaceae family.* Asian J. Microbial. Biotechnology. Environmental. Science. 2007; 9 (1): 177-180.

7. Balandrin, M.J. and Klocke,J.A.*Medicinal, aromatic and industrial materials from plants.* Biotechnology in Agriculture and Forestry Medicinal and Aromatic Plant. Heidelberg: Springer-Verlag; 1988, pp. 1-36.

8. Senthil Kumar, K.L., Mohsin Hassan Mustapha, Anupam Rajbhandari and Ramakrishnan, R. *Phytochemical and Pharmacological Studies on Achillea Millefolium (L) Leaves.* Research Journal of Pharmaceutical, Biological and Chemical Sciences 2011, 2(1)25-30.

9. Isabel Sampaio-Santosa, M., Auxiliadora, M. and KaplanC. *Biosynthesis Significance of Iridoids in Chemosystematics* Journal of the Brazilian Chemical Society, 2001, 12, 2, 144-153

10. Junior, P. *Recent developments in the isolation and structure elucidation of naturally occurring iridoid compounds.* Planta Medica. 1990, *56*, 1.

11. Inouye, H. and Usutu,S. *Progress in the Chemistry of Organic Natural Products.* 1986, *50*, 169, Springer-Verlag, New York.

12. Damtoft, S., Franzyk, H. and Jensen,S.R. *Biosynthesis of iridoids in Forsythia spp.* Phytochemistry 1994, 37, 173–178.

13. Kikuchi, M., Yamauchi, Y., Takahashi, Y., Nagaoka, I. and Sugiyama, M. *Structures of new secoiridoids from the leaves of Syringa vulgaris Linn.* Yakugaku Zasshi 1988.108, 355–360.

14. Inouye,H. *Pharmacognosy and Phytochemistry*, 1971, Springer-Verlag, New York.

15. Harborone, J.B., Baxter, H. and Moss,G.P.*Phytochemical dictionary, Hand Book of bio active Compounds from plants*, 1999, Second (ed). London, Tayolr & Francis.

16. Harborne, J.B. and Mabry,T.J.*The Flavonoids*; Advances in Research, Chapman and Hall, 1982, 1.

17. Wagner, H.*Comparative Phytochemistry*, Acadamic press, London 1996, 309.

18. Adinarano, D. and Rajasekar Rao, R.*Method to distinguish O-Glycosylation and C-Glycosylation in Natural product.* Indian Journal of Chemical Education. 1974, (4) 2, 27.

19. Fylaktakidou, K. C., Hadjipavlou-Litina, D. J., Litinas K. E. and Nicolaides D. N. *Natural and synthetic coumarin derivatives with anti-inflammatory/ antioxidant activities* Current Pharmarmaceutical Design. 2004, 10,3813.
20. Borges, F., Roleira, F., Milhazes, N., Santana, L. and Uriarte,E.*Simple coumarins and analogues in medicinal chemistry: occurrence, synthesis and biological activity.* Current Medicinal Chemistry. 2005, 12,887.

21. Lacy, A. and O'Kennedy,R. *Studies on Coumarins and Coumarin-Related Compounds to Determine their Therapeutic Role in the Treatment of Cancer.* Current Pharmarmaceutical Design 2004, 10, 3797.

22. Borges, F., Roleira, F., Milhazes, N., Uriarte, E., and Santana,L. *Simple coumarins: Privileged Scaffolds in Medicinal Chemistry.* Frontiers in Medicinal Chemistry. 2009, *4*, 23-85.

23. Campos-Toimil, M., Orallo, F., Santana, L. and Uriarte,E. *Synthesis and Vasorelaxant Activity of New Coumarin and Furocoumarin Derivatives. Bioorganic Medicinal* Chemistry *Letters.* 2002, *12*,783-786.

24. Haworth,R.D.*Natural Resins.* Annual Reports on the Progress of Chemistry, 1936, 33: 266

25. Haworth,R.D. *The Chemistry of the Lignan Group of Natural Products.* Journal of Chemical Society, 1942,448.

26. Gottlieb, O.R. *Chemosystematics of the Lauraceae.* Phytochemistry, 1972, 11: 1537

27. Gottlieb, O.R. Neolignans. In: Herz W, Grisebach H, Kirby GW (eds.) *Progress in the Chemistry of Organic Natural Products,* 1978, 35, 1. Springer-Verlag, Vienna.

28. Rao,C.B.S. *Chemistry of Lignans.* 1978, Andhra University Press, Visakhapatnam, India.

29. Hearon, W.M. and McGregor,W.S.*The Naturally Occurring Lignans.* Chemical Review. 1955, 55: 957

30. Stevenson,R.*Some Aspects of Chemistry of Lignans.* Studies in Natural Products Chemistry, 1995, 17, 311. Elsevier, Amsterdam.

31. Arnone, A., Merlini, L. and Zanarotti, A.*Constituents of Silybum marianum. Structure of Isosilybin and Stereochemistry of Silybin.* Journal of Chemical Society, Chemical Communication, 1979, 696.

32. Cooper, R., Gottlieb, H.E. and Lavie,D. *A New Flavolignan of Biogenetic Interest from Aegilop sovata L.*-Part I. Israel Journal of Chemistry, 1977, 16, 12.

33. Ali, Z., Tanaka, T., Iliya, I., Iinuma, M., Furusawa, M., Ito, T., Nakaya, K. and Murata J and Darnaedi D. *Phenolic Constituents of Gnetum kossii.* Journal of Natural Products, 2003, 66: 558.

34. Yao, C., Lin, M. and Wang,L. *Isolation and Biomimetic Synthesis of Anti-inflammatory Stilbenolignans from Gnetum cleistostachyum.* Chemical Pharmaceutical Bulliten, 2006, 54: 1053.

35. Kulesh, N.I., Denisenko, V.A. and Maksimov,O.B. *Stilbenolignan from Maackia amurensis.* 1995, Phytochemistry 40: 1001.

36. Hesse,M. *Alkaloid Chemistry*, 1981, John Wiley & Sons, Newyork.

37. Maier, U.H., Rodl, W., Deus-Neumann, B. and Zenk,M.H. *Biosynthesis of Erythrina alkaloids in Erythrina crista-galli.* Phytochemistry, 1999, 52, 373–382.

38. Dos Santos, R.I., Schripsema, J. and Verpoorte,R. *Ajmalicine metabolism in Catharanthus roseus cell cultures.* Phytochemistry, 1994, 35, 677–681.

39. Gruen, S., Frey, M. and Gierl,A. *Evolution of the indole alkaloid biosynthesis in the genus Hordeum*: Distribution of gramine and DIBOA and isolation of the benzoxazinoid biosynthesis genes from *Hordeum lechleri.* Phytochemistry, 2005, 66,1264–1272.

40. Patterson, S. and O'Hagan,D. 2002, *Biosynthetic studies on the tropane alkaloid hyoscyamine in Daturastramonium*, Phytochemistry, 2002,

61,323–329.

41. Hostettmann, K. and Marston,A. *Saponins*, 1995, Cambridge University Press, Cambridge.

42. Vincken, J.P., Heng, L., de Groot, A. and Gruppen,H. *Saponins, classification and occurrence in the plant kingdom.* Phytochemistry 2007, 68: 275-297.

43. Basu, N. *and* Rastogi,R.P. *Triterpenoid saponins and sapogenins.* Phytochemistry, 1967, 6: 1249-1270.

44. Guclu-ustundag, O. and Mazza,G. *Saponins: Properties, Applications and Processing.* Critical Reviews in Food Science and Nutrition, 2007, 47: 231-258.

45. Rao andGurfinkel. *The bioactivity of saponins: triterpenoid and steroidal glycosides.* Drug Metabolism and Drug Interactions, **2000**, 17:211-235.

46. Lacaille-Dubois,M.A. *Bioactive saponins with cancer related and immunomodulatory activity*: Recent developments. Studies in Natural Products Chemistry. 2005. 32(12): 209–246.

47. Sparg, S.G., Light, M.E. and Van Staden, J. *Biological activities and distribution of plant saponins.* Journal of Ethnopharmacology, 2004. 94(2–3): 219–243.

48. Bachran. C., Bachran, S., Sutherland, M., Bachran, D. and Fuchs,H. *Saponins in tumor therapy.* Mini-Reviews in Medicinal Chemistry, 2008. 8: 575-584.

49. Lacaille-Dubois, M.A. *In Saponins in Food, Feedstuffs and Medicinal Plants* pp. 205-218. 2000, Kluwer Academic Publishers: Pays-Bas.

50. Sato, K.K, Wachino, J., Kondo, T., Ito, H. and Arakawa,Y. *Correlation between reduced susceptibility to disinfectants and Multidrug resistance among clinical isolates of Acinetobacter species* Journal of Antimicrobial Chemotherapy, 2010, 24: 1-9.

51. Blois,M. *Antioxidant determination by the use of stable free radical.* Nature, 1958, 181, 1199-1200.

52. Marcocci, L., Packer, L., Sckaki, A. and Albert,G.M.,*Antioxidant action of Ginkgo biloba extracts.* Methods in Enzymology, 1994, 234, 462-475.

53. Cooper, G.M. *The Cancer Book.* Jones and Bartlett Publishers, Boston, M.A 1993, 7.

54. Pezzuto, J.M. *Plant-derived anticancer agents.* Biochem. Pharmacol. 1997, 53, 121-133.

55. Cragg, G. M., Newman, D. J. and Snader, K.M. *Natural Products as Sources of New Drugs over the Period 1981-2002.* J. Nat. Prod. 2003, 66, 1022-37.

56. Joseph C Maroon, Jeffrey W Bost and Adara Maroon . *Natural anti-inflammatory agents for pain relief.* Surg Neurol Int, 2010, 1:80.

57. Bruno,I.J, Cole,J.C., Edgington, P.R., Kessler.M., Macrae,C.F,McCabe,P., Pearson,J. and Taylor, R. *New software for searching the Cambridge structural database and visualizing crystal structures.* Acta Crystallogr B, 2002, 58:389–397.

58. SevilÖksüz, Roberto, R., Gil, Thitima Pengsuparp, John, M., Pezzuto, Geoffrey, A. and Cordell. *Four diterpene esters from Euphorbia myrsinites,* Phytochemistry, 1995, 38(6), 1457-1462

59. Chen, K., Shi, Q.A., Fujioka, T., Zhang, D.C., Hu, C.Q., Jin, J, Q., Kilkuskie, R.E. and Lee K.H. *Anti-AIDSagents,Tripterifordin,anovelanti-HIVprinciplefromTripterygiumwilfordii:isolation and structural elucidation.* Journal of Natural Product. 1992, 55(1):88-92.

60. Bakkali, F., Averbeck, S., Averbeck, D.S, Idaoman,M. *Biological effects of essential oils.* Food and Chemical Toxicology, 2008, 46; 2, 446-475.

61. Chang, R.S., Ding, L., Chen, G. Q., Pan, Q. C., Zhao, Z. L. and Smith, K. M. *Dehydroandro grapholide Succinic Acid Monoester as an Inhibitor against the Human Immunodeficiency Virus.* Proceeding Society of Experimental

Biology and Medicine.1991, *197*, 59-66.

62. Yu, D., Suzuki, M., Xie, L., Morris-Natschke, S.L. and Lee, K.H. *Recent progress in the development of coumarin derivatives as potent anti-HIV agents* Medicinal. Research. Review. 2003, 23, 322-345.

63. Q.T., Bernard,P. Reverse pharmacognosy: *a new concept for accelerating natural drug discovery,* Lead Molecules from Natural Products.2006, Elsevier, 1–20.

64. Duke, J.A. *Handbook of Phytochemical Constituents of GRASH erbsand Other Economic Plants*.1992,CRC Press, BocaRaton.

www.ingramcontent.com/pod-product-compliance
Ingram Content Group UK Ltd.
Pitfield, Milton Keynes, MK11 3LW, UK
UKHW021925190726
13853UKWH00002B/853

9 798889 090861